the architecture of **will bruder**

ORO Editions
Publishers of Architecture, Art, and Design
Gordon Goff: Publisher

www.oroeditions.com
info@oroeditions.com

Published by ORO Editions

Author: Will Bruder
Book concept: Will Bruder
Project Manager for WBA: Richard Bosch
Project Manager: Jake Anderson

Book Design: Pablo Mandel / CircularStudio
Typeset in Helvetica Now

10 9 8 7 6 5 4 3 2 1 First Edition

ISBN: 978-1-961856-76-9

Prepress and Print work by ORO Editions Inc.
Printed in China

ORO Editions makes a continuous effort to minimize the overall carbon footprint of its publications. As part of this goal, ORO, in association with Global ReLeaf, arranges to plant trees to replace those used in the manufacturing of the paper produced for its books. Global ReLeaf is an international campaign run by American Forests, one of the world's oldest nonprofit conservation organizations. Global ReLeaf is American Forests' education and action program that helps individuals, organizations, agencies, and corporations improve the local and global environment by planting and caring for trees.

the architecture of **will bruder**

Acknowledgments

Many heads, hearts, and hands have made this book possible.

The gift of supportive parents nurtured my explorations of materials and making. On long family car trips saw the United States up close, through a windshield and a camera lens. Public education opportunities offered in Milwaukee, Wisconsin, were foundational: **Miss Timm**, my challenging fifth grade teacher; the **Fisher Body Craftsman's Guild** model car competitions in high school; work/study at the **General Motors Institute** in Flint, Michigan—all these set me on a design path. The **University of Wisconsin-Milwaukee** allowed me to cobble together work, study, and travel while pursuing my undergraduate degree. There I met my former wife, **Simon Bruder**, who supported my goals for many years.

The opportunity to "learn by doing" at **William Wenzler**'s studio, to immerse myself in the studio's library, to work side by side with Wenzler's team, especially his self-educated, gifted designer, **Michael P. Johnson**, all of these gave me the wings and confidence to pursue my dream. Time with maverick architects **Gunnar Birkerts**, **Bruce Goff**, and most importantly, the visionary **Paolo Soleri**, honed my understanding of architecture and its possibilities. Pre-licensure apprenticeships with **Warner Design for Business**, and architects **James Lakin**, **Florence & Walling**, and **Kemper** and **Michael Goodwin** grounded me in place and practice and let me see, firsthand, the results of my design efforts. **Paul Schweikher Sr.**, in his Arizona years, mentored me in ways beyond words.

When I first hung out my shingle, small projects came by word of mouth and good local press. Since then clients, public and private, large and small, have come, trusting me with their aspirations and resources. My **studio colleagues and support staff** have all joined their heads, hearts and hands to realize architecture. They have challenged me with their fresh ideas, attitudes and abilities. I am gratified that many now fly on strong wings.

The realization of architecture depends on collaboration with skilled **craftspeople**, **fabricators**, **consultants**, and **contractors**. Time and again, often on the job site, we have challenged each other with this question: Is there an opportunity to make the ordinary into the extraordinary? Often, together, we have found a way. They have taught me so much, and I share any success I have had with them.

Scott and **Debbie Jarson**, tireless advocates for Arizona architecture, have been in my "sidecar" advising and supporting and enabling my sometimes eccentric and romantic ideas for the last forty years.

On the last projects, my esteemed colleague **Bob Neely**, principal of Lamar Johnson Collaborative, has been an extraordinary partner and friend.

The "building" of this book has required another set of skills, time, and talent, all beyond my understanding. Foundational is the ever-patient book designer/architect **Richard Bosch**, and my studio assistant **Salix Sampson**, both Portland based. Arizona-based photographer **Bill Timmerman** has been at my side for years. He has worked his magic, and made valued suggestions, on the photos herein. **Tim Hursley**'s photographs have always brought a fresh eye and attitude, while **Friends of Kebyar** supported early documentation of the work. **Harold Housley**, Archivist at the Arizona State University, Design and Arts Library, continues to skillfully and tirelessly archive the studio's work.

The book would not exist without the carefully crafted, thoughtful, and provocative essays of valued architecture **colleagues** and **friends**. Their words give voice to my efforts over the past fifty years. I am honored by your contributions. **Jack DeBartolo III**, **Wendell Burnette**, and **Kent McClure**, former studio mates, have been diligent in their advocacy for this monograph. They have offered valued input, facilitated essay contributions and made the introduction to ORO Editions. ORO, in turn, has generously guided this process with candor, content suggestions, and layout and editorial assist to make this book possible.

And finally, thanks to my partner in love and life, **Louise Roman**, for being by my side for the past 20-plus years.

Table of Contents

post Rome projects: 1986-2025

appendix

Preface: Will Bruder

A ride on my new bicycle at age eleven planted a seed that would grow over the next fifty years. In the summer of 1957, I was exploring the surround of my family's new home on the western suburban edge of Milwaukee, Wisconsin, where I was born and raised and spent my formative years. On that ride, I crossed the allowable boundaries my parents had set. There, behind an unsecured fence, was Frank Lloyd Wright's Greek Orthodox Church in Wauwatosa, Wisconsin, still under construction. With its circular plan geometry and domed concrete roof already in place, it was unlike anything I had ever seen in my young life!

Milwaukee was a good place to be coming of age at that time. While many deserted the near-in downtown where my father still worked as a fireman, some, like our three-generation family, moved to the city's edge where new schools in burgeoning communities were opening.

Frank Lloyd Wright's Greek Orthodox Church under construction in 1960[1]

Eero Saarinen's Milwaukee War Memorial Museum in 1967[2]

The three I attended were in the style and manner of the young Eero Saarinen's inventive Crow Island School of 1940: simple in their one-story configurations of expressed brick masonry, with large glass walls protected by deep overhangs. Memorably, Miss Timm, my extraordinary 5th grade teacher, invited me to look with her out those generous windows and comment on what I saw with a crayon ink resist drawing. It was the first time I had considered "the window," "the view."

Eero Saarinen's 1957 Milwaukee War Memorial Center/Art Museum, as well, made a deep impression on me. Its robust cantilevered concrete galleries thrust off the east-facing park bluff and overlooked Lake Michigan and the horizon beyond.

My father, the son of a German cabinetmaker and a very competent woodworker himself, returned from his service in World War II in the 82nd Airborne, and signed on to a be a City of Milwaukee firefighter, while my mother was a dime store clerk. My father's generous "off hours" meant we spent lots of time together in the basement. It was full of well-used tools and afforded us the space to work together on an elaborate "to scale" train/city layout in one corner.

I was an only child, asthmatic, with no interest, like my father, in athletics. We were totally "in sync" on making things. Junior high school shop classes in wood and metalworking, along with technical drafting, would totally capture and inspire my imagination. Ambitious family road trips ranging from two-four weeks duration across the US, to East and West Coast cities as well as a network of national parks and monuments. These travels offered me a window on a wider world.

My interest in design with a capital D was catalyzed by Fisher Body Auto Design Competitions that were announced at a boys-only assembly at my middle school. I signed up right away and for $2.50 received the instructions and four "to scale" rubber wheels from which I would make a series of to scale futuristic car models, working up from plasticine clay studies to carved and shaped laminated wood block, with untold coats of auto paint. For the rubber tires provided in the kit, I fashioned aluminum hub caps of my own design. Over the next four years, my models progressed from third place "in state" to the top "regional prize" in 1963.

With the regional prize came a full week of immersion in all things General Motors in Detroit including time at the nearby GM Technical Center by Eero Saarinen. Fifty-five boys, all Fisher Body competition regional winners, from across the country, were issued sports coats with an elaborate insignia for formal assemblies and site visits on this trip. Over that week we saw the next year's cars coming around the GM test track. We also attended a Tigers baseball game and took a trip to Stratford, Ontario, Canada, to see Shakespeare's *The Taming of the Shrew.*

Thus, by the end of high school, and after lots and lots of shop and mechanical drawing classes, I begin to think that maybe car design would be my future. I had no money to attend Art Center College in Pasadena, California, which was a prestigious pipeline to a career in auto design. However, I was sponsored to attend in Flint, Michigan, the General Motors Institute (GMI), cooperative work/study program. My parents were overjoyed and gifted me a new 1964 silver Corvair coupe as a high school graduation present. Cars were us!

I drove to Flint and spent about nine months in the program, splitting time between the factory floor of my sponsor and classes. I lived in the attic guest suite of the widow of a GM union organizer and, indeed shamefully, crossed picket lines, as the plant where I was assigned was on strike. These nine months were enough for me to know this was not for me.

My parents were crestfallen when I announced that I was leaving the GMI program.

Recalling the formative experiences with making and materials and my exposure to and curiosity about architecture, I decided that architecture was to be my next career pursuit. I would get a summer job with an architect and, while living at home, cobble together a course of study at the University of Wisconsin-Milwaukee that might support my ambition. The only "architecture school" in Wisconsin at the time was Frank Lloyd Wright's Taliesin, and I could not afford Mies van der Rohe's Illinois Institute of Technology in Chicago. Neither would have been a good fit for me anyway.

Back home in Milwaukee I got VERY lucky! 1). Given the Vietnam War was in full rage, I was called up by the draft board but received a 1Y deferment, with my long history of asthma, and my only child status, working in my favor. 2). The next week at a Sunday evening dinner of a church friend, my host Mr. Terry asked me what I was going to do over that summer. I said, "Tomorrow I am going to go through the yellow pages of the phone book and land a job with an architect." Mr. Terry said, "Well I know someone, through Scouts, a very good man, who is an architect. His name is William Wenzler, and he might be helpful."

Will Bruder Fisher Body Craftsmen Guild Design Competition Prize Winning model cars[3]

The next morning, very early, I drove to Wenzler's office in the Milwaukee suburbs. I was waiting on his studio doorstep with my small portfolio of drawings and a couple of my Fisher Body model cars under my arm. He graciously invited me in. After taking a look at my offerings, he said, "Do you want to start now or next week?" I said, "Now."

Little did I know that I would be part of one of the most progressive and dynamic modernist architectural studios in Wisconsin, led by Wenzler, a University of Illinois architectural school graduate, whose work was supported by a talented team of architects, draftsmen, and an in house structural engineer. In the studio Michael Johnson took me under his wing and encouraged me to join the Seven Arts Book Club. With the help of my family and friends, whose memberships I subsidized, I got seven books for each membership. It was the start of my personal arts and architecture library. In addition, I became Michael's evening assistant on his moonlighting "side jobs." Wenzler's studio was cranking out exceptional work. Learning through doing was powerful. Neal Krueger introduced me to stories about Arizona —where his parents published the magazine *Arizona Highways* via Krueger Lithography. I took advantage of the studio's well-stocked architectural book and periodical library.

Top: carved concrete sculpture
Bottom: carved plaster sculptures
Both from UW–Milwaukee BFA sculpture studio classes 1964-1969[3]

For the next five years, I attended the University of Wisconsin-Milwaukee (where the tuition was $130 per semester) and worked part time or full time at Wenzler's. Fascination with Arizona was percolating in the studio and emboldened me to ask for a summer off to attend the Silt Pile 7 workshop at the visionary architect Paolo Soleri's Cosanti studio. While there, I even received college credit from Arizona State University that transferred to the University of Wisconsin-Milwaukee!

During that hot Arizona summer of 1967, I stayed at the old Doubletree Inn where Soleri had secured cheap housing for out-of-towners like me. I was drawn to Soleri's ideas and inventive processes. I explored the area, including the ruins of the Upton House in Scottsdale, a house commissioned by a Chicago industrialist, designed by architect Paul Schweikher Sr., and built by George Ellis. I was totally enthralled by its remaining skeletal forms of stone, concrete, and wood, as well as the play of light on this ruin. I started to track Schweikher in the architectural press, to good result.

Back in Milwaukee that fall, my coursework at UWM focused on basic design, sculpture, drawing, and calligraphy, with studios in metal and ceramics. A full suite of art history classes was complemented by a heavy dose of structural engineering.

In January of 1967, I married my art studio classmate, Simon, at a small family wedding at Wright's Unitarian Meeting House in Madison, Wisconsin. We immediately set out in my Corvair on a six-month art and architecture road trip that would meander from Wisconsin across America back to Soleri's Cosanti Foundation. Our stops included every Wright and Bruce Goff building along the way. After researching his address at the local library, we knocked on the door of Goff's house in Kansas City, Missouri. He greeted us with, "You must be the Bruders. I have been expecting you." A wide-ranging discussion of architecture followed and ended, near midnight, with us listening to the music of Olivier Messiaen, one of his favorite composers. The next day, Goff's clients generously opened their homes to us, and spoke with gratitude about their collaboration with Goff, which was evidenced by the loving care of their wonderfully inventive homes.

For the next nine months, back in Arizona, Simon and I apprenticed to Soleri, living in a trailer on the Cosanti site. It was an exciting time. Paolo was writing his *Arcology: The City in the Image of Man*, while building 3D city models, and planning to test his ideas at a prototype city, "Arcosanti," on land he had purchased in the high desert, ninety miles to the north of Cosanti. Paolo's work caught the spirit of the 1960s. Lots of folks, including Buckminster Fuller, and even Jimi Hendrix and Richie Havens, passed through that spring. Though never a "hippie," I grew my hair long and my beard out, as was the style back then.

On return to Milwaukee that fall, Simon and I finished our coursework. I graduated with a BFA, with a major in sculpture and a minor in structural engineering.

I was confident that my background would equip me to get a job as an apprentice in an architect's studio. Toronto held much promise, and I got offers from three well-regarded firms: Macy DuBois, Ron Thom, and John Andrews. But transferable architectural licensing complications pointed me towards my last stop in the US: the studio of Gunnar Birkerts Architects in Birmingham, Michigan, a near-in suburb of Detroit. Birkerts was a protégé of Eero Saarinen. I landed a position as a designer in Birkerts's studio. My year there was memorable. I worked on the design and construction documents, as well as job supervision, of the Contemporary Arts Museum Houston. Seeing that project through all architectural phases to built reality was to be truly formative.

But after another punishingly cold year in the Upper Midwest, Simon and I decided to head back to Arizona, where I would seek work as an architect's apprentice and Simon would pursue her advanced degrees in archeology at ASU.

I was again very fortunate to quickly make some strong connections with designers and architectural studios who had lots of work and gave me design opportunities. My long hair, and admittedly my audacious approach, did not sit well with some, but my studio experiences with Warner's Design for Business and architects James Lakin, Florence & Walling, and Kemper and Michael Goodwin were significantly formative.

With Goodwin, I would lead design efforts on both Cherokee Elementary School and the Paradise Valley Town Hall. I got to know contractors, suppliers, and master craftsmen, and I looked at all the work that was coming out of the ground from other studios in Phoenix and beyond.

One afternoon, while still at Florence & Walling, I heard a chance conversation some distance from my board. It would lead to one of the most important relationships in my life. A former F&W employee owned a blueprint shop in Sedona, Arizona. He was regaling his former studio mates with the story of an older architect, with a German-sounding name, who was bringing to his shop for printing amazing drawings of a house he was building for himself and his wife outside Sedona. I quickly joined the conversation and asked if the architect's name might be Paul Schweikher. "Yes, that is it," was his reply!

I had seen Schweikher's work in the architectural press, as well as the ruins of his Upton House in Scottsdale. I was burning with curiosity. The next week, on the way back from a job site visit in Flagstaff, Arizona, I drove down Oak Creek Canyon to Sedona, looking for a view of this house. On a distant bluff I saw a structure that was very distinctive, so I drove towards it. I found the driveway attached to a remarkable house and made my way up to it. The structure had no apparent front door. Instead, there was a breezeway to a covered open-air deck. I was overwhelmed by the originality and mastery in wood of this home, with its simple black corrugated metalwork capping a long gable. Standing in awe for some time, my attention was broken by the opening of a sliding, clear Plexiglas door. I was greeted with a smile by an elderly gentleman. I said, "Are you Paul Schweikher? I thought you were

Top: wire sculpture
Bottom: cast metal sculptures
Both from UW–Milwaukee BFA sculpture studio classes 1964–1969[3]

dead." Not a great opener, right? Then again, many people had come to gawk at the house and knock on the door, but none had addressed him by his full name. And so began our twenty-plus year friendship and mentorship, this being only the first of my many visits and overnights at Paul and Dorothy Schweikher's house. My deep investigation and appreciation of Schweikher's life and work, and its evolution over the years, will be contained in a forthcoming monograph titled *Paul Schweikher Architect: A Master of Design and Making*.

In 1973 I completed my apprenticeship requirements and prepared for my licensing examinations. I passed them on first try and hung out my shingle in February of 1974. My "studio," with one drafting board, was in a small fifty-square-foot annex I had built onto our garden/courtyard apartment. Jobs started to come in, mostly modest remodels, additions, and patio reworks. My clients liked the results of our efforts together and spread the word. Some had connections to the local press, which I soon learned was hungry for content. As well, I established a relationship with *Sunset Home & Garden Magazine*.

While never an advocate of Soleri's Arcosanti experiment in Cordes Junction, Arizona, nor an apprentice at Wright's Taliesin West, a desert building site of my own design held allure. I had jobs to the south and north of Phoenix and could drive to the Schweikhers' house in Sedona on weekends via unclogged roads. With the help, again, of my parents, who had retired to Sun City, Arizona, I purchased a ten-acre site for $10,000 on the east side of Daisy Mountain in New River, Arizona.

There I designed a modest +/-800-square-foot live/work space, carefully siting the structure to optimize views and mitigate the hot summer sun. I built the structure in about five weeks with the help of skilled and like-minded friends and colleagues. I understood the power of the press, the spirit of the time, and Arizona's place in it. When the house won Architectural Record Houses of the Year in 1977, architects and others took notice.

At some point I became aware of the American Academy in Rome and the Rome Prize Fellowship in Architecture. I set my sights on applying when I turned 40. Antoine Predock came back from his time in Rome and strongly encouraged me to apply, as did others. To supplement my application, I crafted an accordion book of images with a text narrative running across the bottom of each page.

When I received word of the Fellowship award, my studio mates stepped up and carried projects on between my brief return trips to Arizona.

My light-filled American Academy studio overlooked Rome. It afforded me time to reflect, travel, and directly experience so many works that I had only seen in publications. Carlo Scarpa's work, in particular, made an indelible impact.

Although there already had been discernible threads in the projects presented in this monograph, the Rome experience shifted and deepened the way I saw the world and my work. That visceral experience underpins the organizational strategy of this book into a selection of pre-Rome and post-Rome projects.

Credits

(1) Construction view showing front of Annunciation Greek Orthodox Church, Wauwautosa, WI (Frank Lloyd Wright, Architect). Photograph by John Underhill Ottenheimer, November 1960. Image courtesy Organic Architecture + Design Archives/John Underhill Ottenheimer Papers. Used with permission, all rights reserved.

(2) Photograph by Alan Band/Fox Photos October 1967 Image courtesy of Wisconsin Historical Society, WHI-53921.

(3) Photo Credit: Will Bruder Studio.

Working to Scale—My Design Process

My design process is critically grounded in 'listening' to the site, and listening to the programmatic needs of clients, be they individuals, families, communities or companies.

The best design solutions depend not merely on form, space, or image, but upon the more holistic consideration of an inside/out, outside/in design process.

I start every project with no preconceptions as to the architectural solution. Topographic plans and sections are made. If the site is 'complicated,' three-dimensional site models are constructed.

Each element of the program is assigned a 'to-scale' paper square, which is then placed on the site.

This dynamic pre-design tool creates a series of flexible opportunities as I move the 'to-scale' parts and pieces around the site and achieve the square footage allowed by the budget. These 'building blocks' energize early, and often multiple, hand drawings that will be the foundation of later schematics.

The ability of the hand drawing to inform, define and test inventions of the mind is unparalleled. A scale drawing can efficiently and elegantly map the macro boundaries of the site's conditions as related to the path of the sun and the flow of surrounding movements. It can capture nuances of topography, axes of connectivity, as well as unexpected framed vistas and intimately scaled atmospheres of an architectural experience.

From refinement of the formal schematic through to the carefully detailed construction document used to guide the maker/craftsman, drawings are always at both the heart and soul of the architect's expression of ideas!

early projects: 1974-1987

Lawson Patios, Phoenix, Arizona, 1976
Matthews Residence, Phoenix, Arizona, 1978, entry

This entry and patio both show the simple integration of structural form, materials, and natural light, which carries through all of Bruder's work.

Photos: © Neil Koppes, unless noted otherwise
Conceptual sketches and presentation drawings: Will Bruder

Will Bruder is an artist/architect who for his first fourteen years worked from a desert studio in New River, Arizona. His work is functional in its acknowledgment of site and user need, craftsmanlike in its concern for detail and building process, and sculptural in its unique blending of space, materials, and light.

Bruder has a bachelor of fine arts degree in sculpture from the University of Wisconsin-Milwaukee and is self-trained as an architect. Besides his formal education, he apprenticed under several significant American architects, including Gunnar Birkerts and Paolo Soleri, and he has also worked in the field, doing carpentry and concrete work. He registered as an architect and opened his own studio in 1974. His years of experience have been a quality pursuit of architecture as art, married to a "hands-on" sense of practical, but poetic, reality.

Over the years, many of Bruder's commissions have been tied to "owner-builder" efforts, and they all celebrate the craft of building in ways not typical in contemporary architecture today.

The noted Italian critic Bruno Zevi has written of Bruder's work:

> *It is then a mixture of organicism ... and deep sensitivity towards the fundamental coherence of the structure, that which Wright used to call "the place and time" ... The gifts of this American architect with his easy manner, technological accuracy, and formal nonconformity are indisputable.*
> *L'Architettura*, May 1980

Bruder's architecture has been widely presented in books and periodicals in the United States, Europe, and Japan. He has won numerous awards and exhibited and lectured widely. In 1987 he received an Advanced Design Fellowship (Rome Prize) from the American Academy in Rome, where he studied for six months.

The following overview of his work will hopefully give a sense of Bruder's philosophy and approach to his art and architecture, which is a celebration of both site and user need, choreographed to stimulate the senses.

The content that makes up this Pre-Rome section is excerpted from: *Friends of Kebyar* 6.1, no. 37 (1988)

Galloway Cabin, Pinewood, Arizona, 1973
Will Bruder Studio/Residence, New River, Arizona, 1975
Karber A/C Offices, Phoenix, Arizona, 1976

Will Bruder Studio, New River, Arizona, 1979, exterior

Will Bruder Studio, New River, Arizona, 1979, studio

Karber Residence, Phoenix, Arizona, 1977. Located on a small urban/suburban site, this home's main design focus is a large brick funnel that opens to the city view and south sun and contains the primary family activities. A series of galvanized metal-clad cylinders serve as bedrooms and service elements, sculpturally complementing the angular forms.

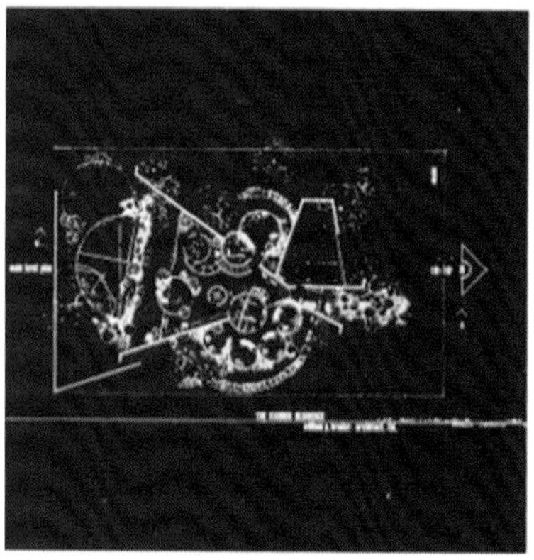

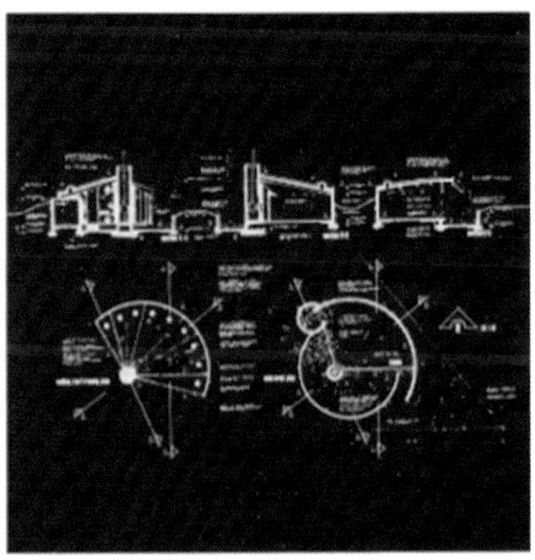

Rotharmel Studio Retreat, Glendale, Arizona, 1975. This circular, precisely crafted, cast-in-place "concrete cave" is set two and a half feet below grade and is entered by crossing a water garden. The various gray textures of the concrete structure are set off by white oak, stainless steel, leather, slabs of glass (set into the concrete without mullions), and lush landscaping. It is a true desert oasis!

Matthews Residence, Phoenix, Arizona, 1978. This Southwestern courtyard home of stabilized mud adobe is sited on a suburban double cul-de-sac lot. The heavy texture of the adobe and rough wood framing contrast with refined elements of galvanized metal and fine oak. A plan geometry of pure curves using multiple center points gives a sense of spatial drama. A strip skylight flowing from entry to living area adds a very dynamic element to the architecture.

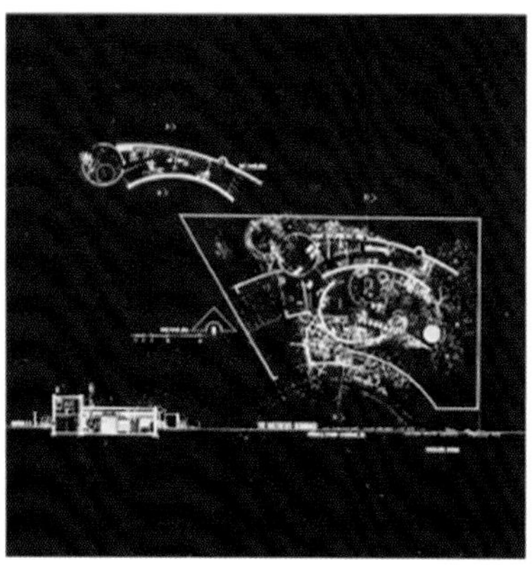

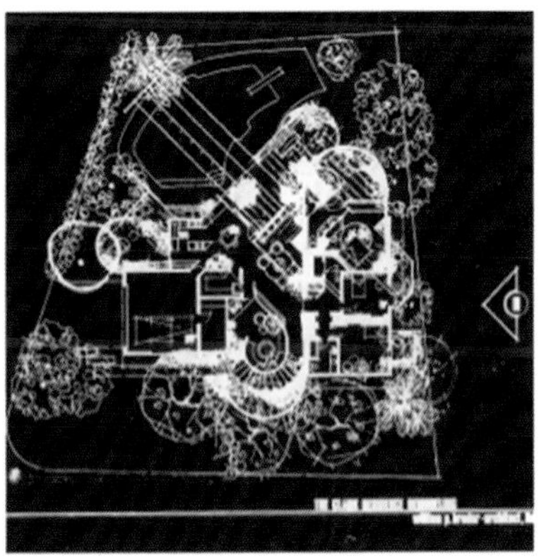

Clark Residence Remodel, Phoenix, Arizona, 1977. This total reworking of an existing 1960s tract home is a sculptural exercise in materials and function. The sandblasted concrete block "8" wall that flows through the existing house gives the new architecture both unity and order. The exquisite white oak and vermillion wood cabinets, stainless-steel walls and doors, and use of natural daylight create unique spatial tensions.

Mesquite Branch Library, Phoenix, Arizona, 1979. This 10,000-square-foot public library uses a simple 45-degree geometry in massing and plan. The main reading room has a very human scale defined by a ceiling of large exposed precast concrete beams, natural resawn fir plywood sheeting, and sculptural galvanized metal ducts. Furnishings, graphics, and artwork selected by the architect give it a sense of design completeness.

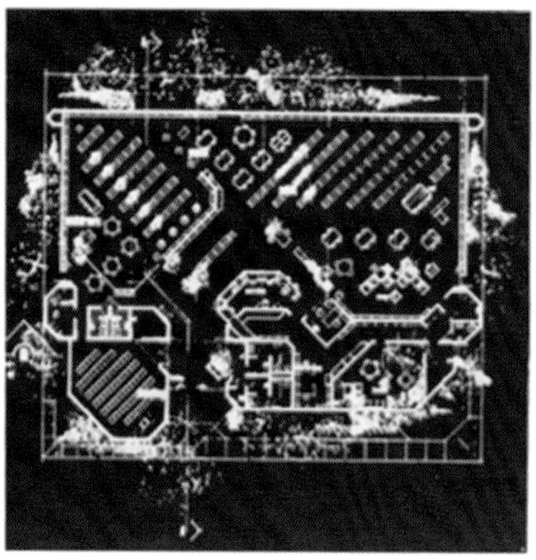

Phoenix Day School for the Deaf, Phoenix, Arizona, 1981. Circles and daylight give character and sparkle to this school complex. A Teflon-coated, fiberglass fabric roof assembly in tension covers the gymnasium. The use of tilt-up exposed concrete walls and simple steel framing provided substantial budget economics.

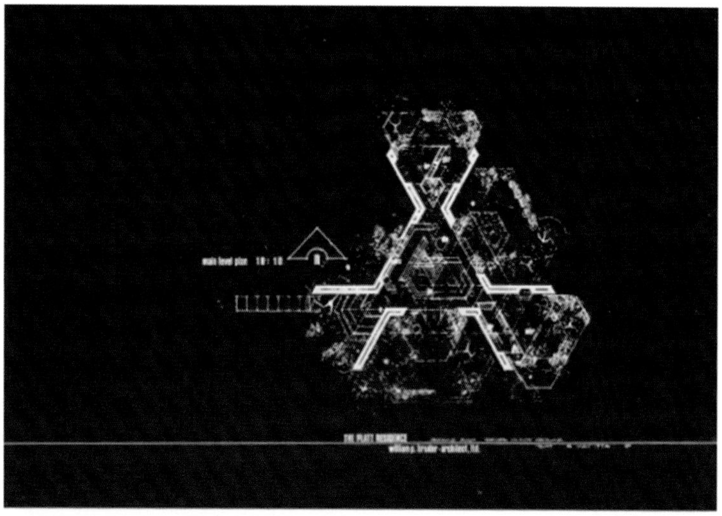

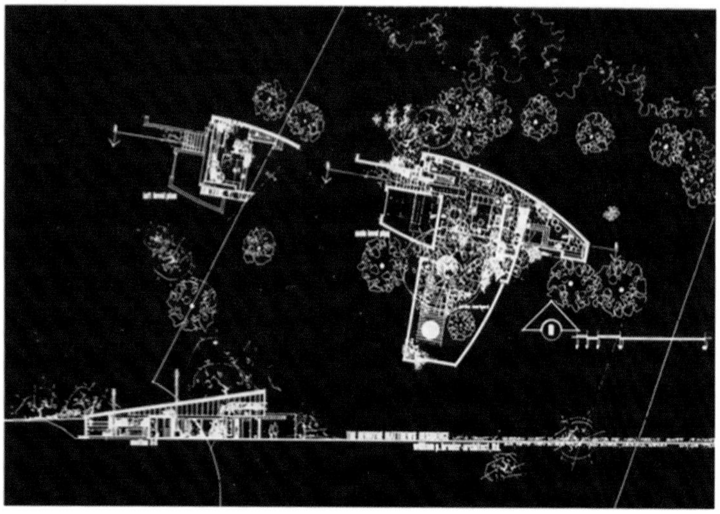

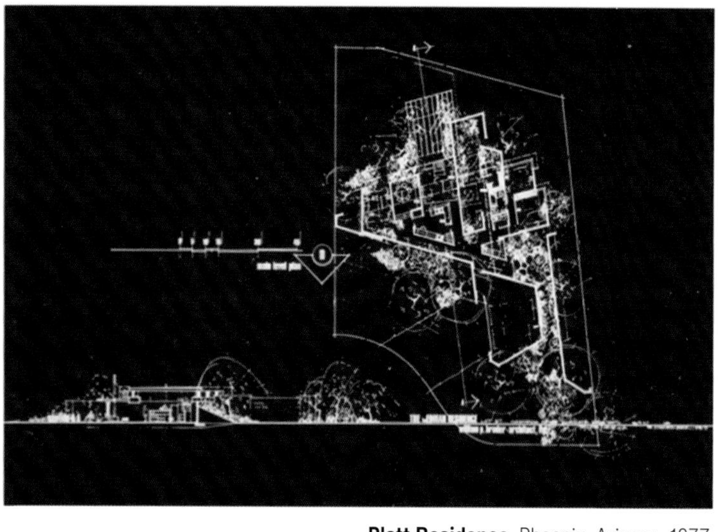

Platt Residence, Phoenix, Arizona, 1977
Dewayne Matthews Residence, Santa Fe, New Mexico, 1980, unbuilt
Redman Residence, Tempe, Arizona, 1983

Photos: Will Bruder, both pages

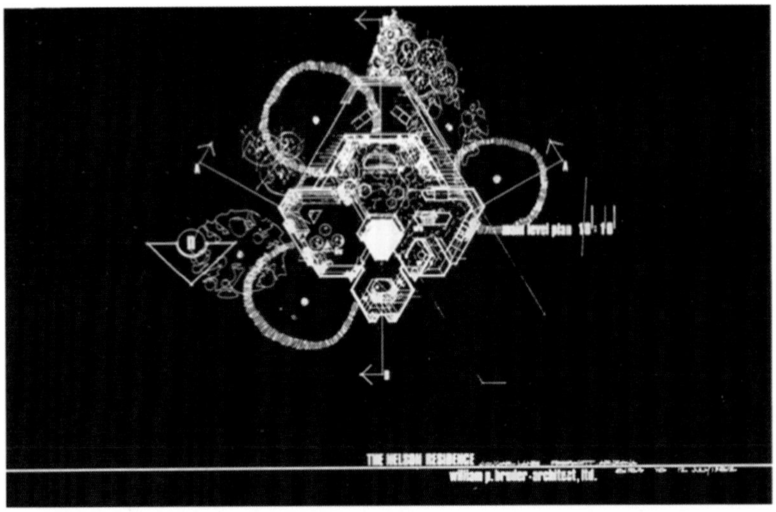

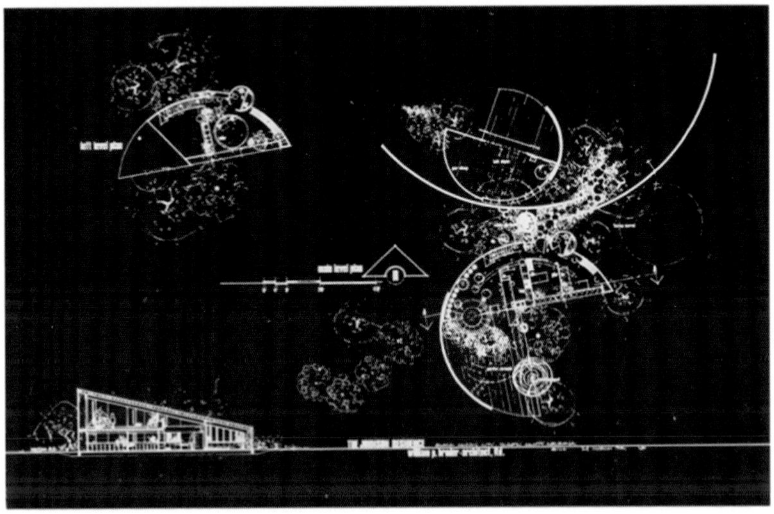

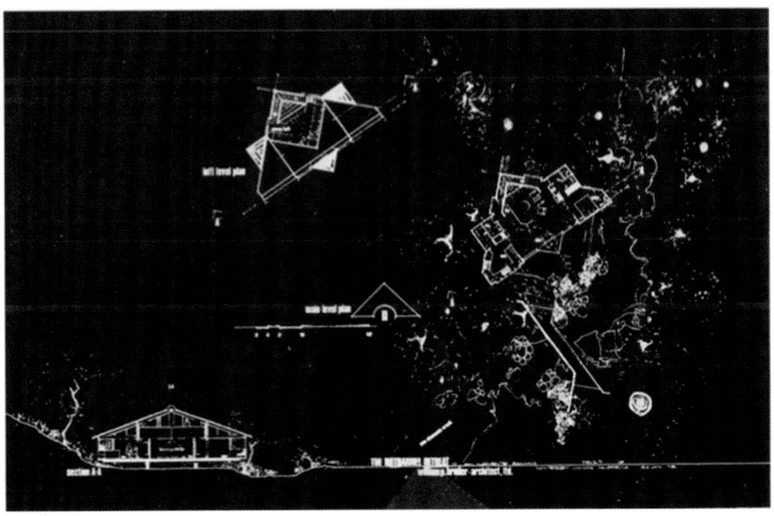

Nelson Residence, Prescott, Arizona, 1981
Johnson Residence, Black Canyon City, Arizona, 1980, unbuilt
Rotharmel Residence, Monterey, California, 1984, unbuilt

Johnston Residence, Phoenix, Arizona, 1979. This structure of concrete, stone, copper, and glass appears to grow from a mountain ridge above the city. A sculptural driveway ramp of concrete is a kinetic focus for the entry to the home. The interiors take full advantage of the views.

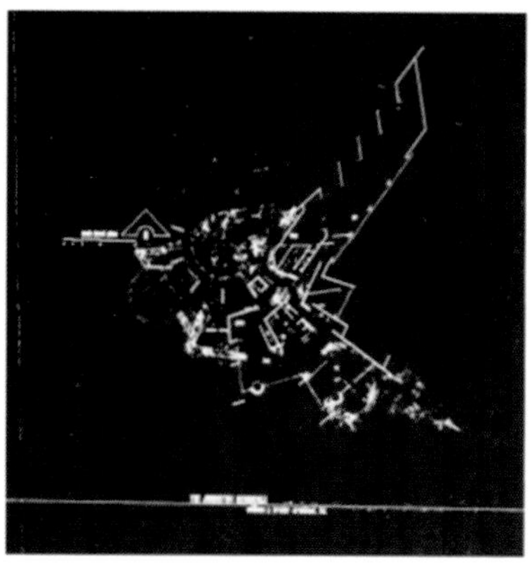

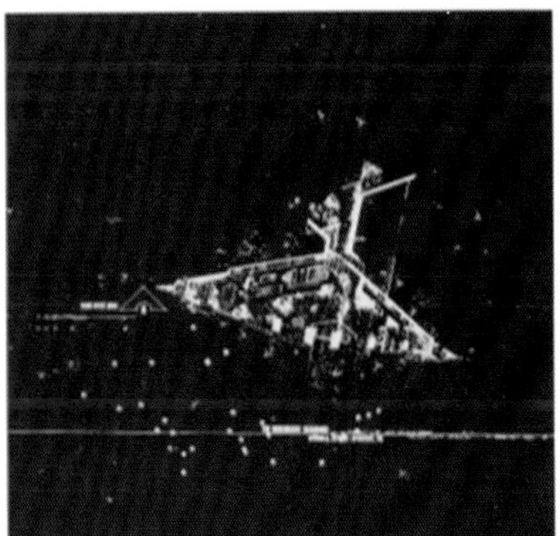

Rosenbaum Residence, Cave Creek, Arizona, 1981. Native stone has been laid with angular precision (apparently mortarless) to form piers and walls that frame views of an undisturbed desert site. Custom weathered steel trusses, copper roofs, and uniform red birch cladding and millwork mesh to create a bold organic statement.

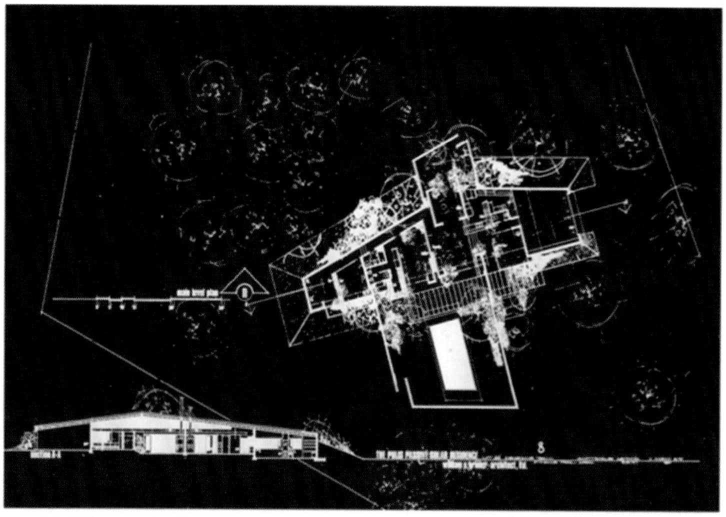

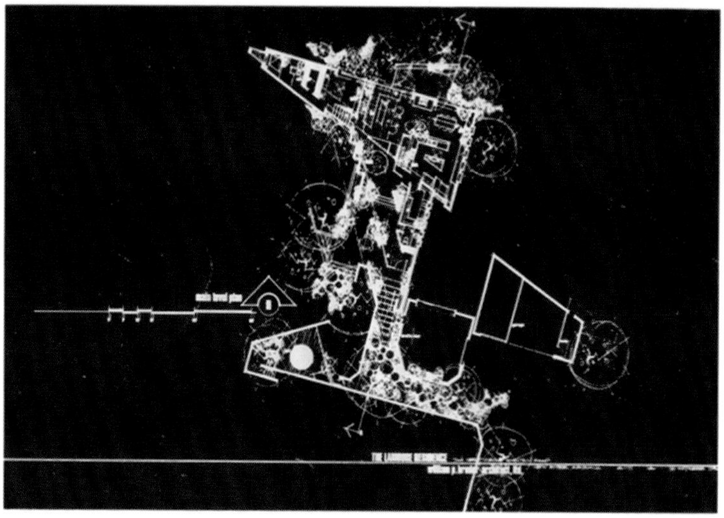

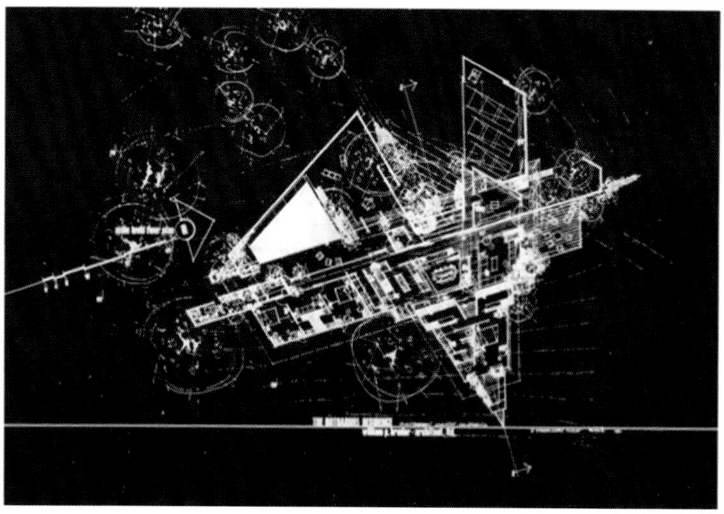

Pulis Residence, Scottsdale, Arizona, 1983
Lamoure Residence, New River, Arizona, 1981
Rotharmel Residence, Monterey, California, 1984

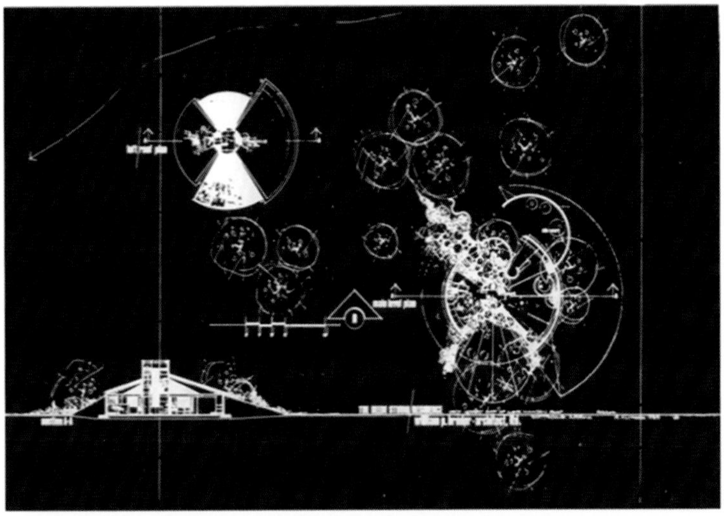

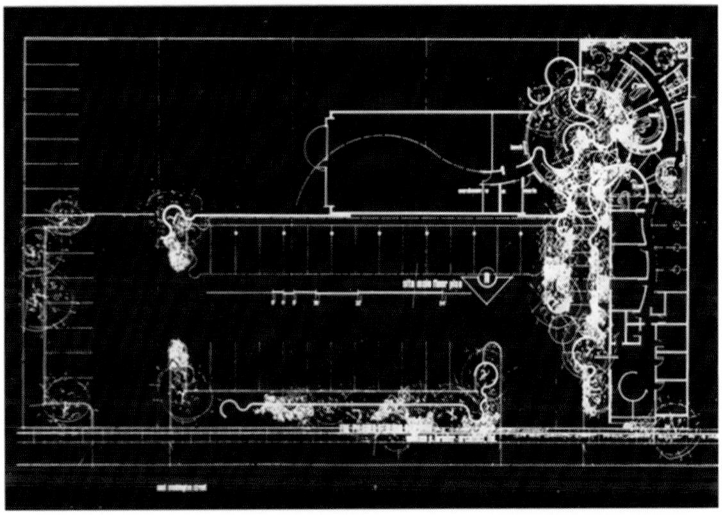

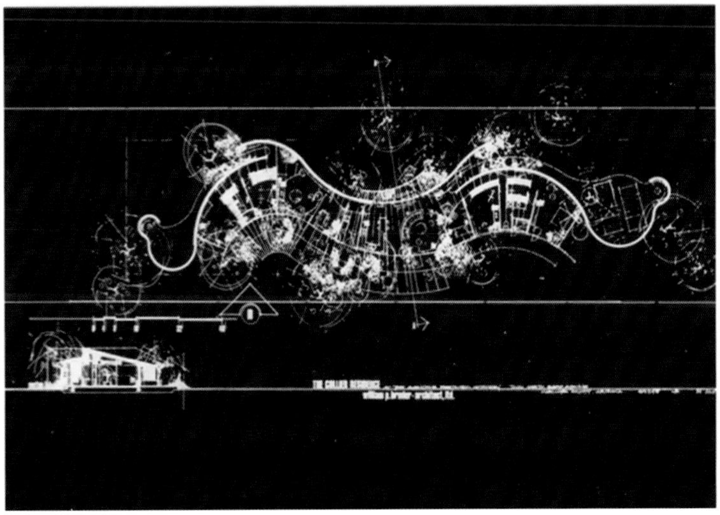

Photo: Will Bruder, bottom

Heede Residence, Scottsdale, Arizona, 1983
Streech Electric Expansion/Pilcher Building, Phoenix, Arizona, 1982
Collier Residence, Phoenix, Arizona, 1985

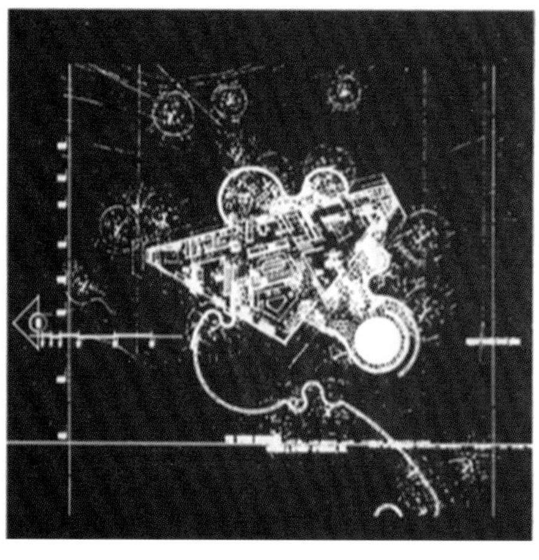

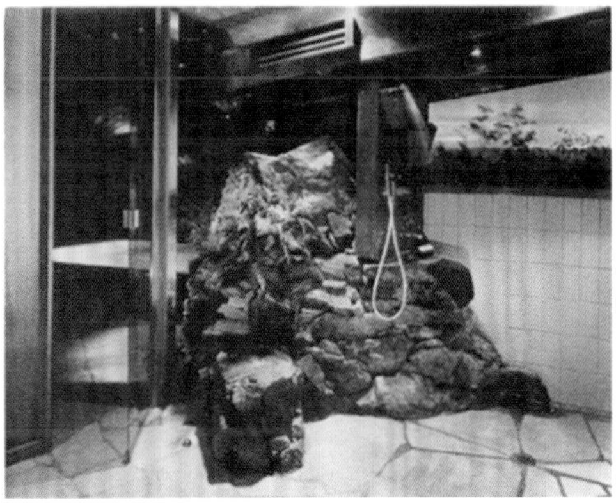

Photos: © Hans Lettner, both pages

Weiss Residence, Paradise Valley, Arizona, 1985. A multi-axis triangular plan geometry allows this cantilevered residence to maximize both views and privacy on its mountainside site. An exterior of naturally patinated copper, green Solex glazing, and stone quarried from the site create an eloquent exterior image. The interior of white oak, resawn spruce, copper, and flagstone with Berber wool carpeting creates a warm and casual background for living. Interiors by the architect feature custom steel and glass tables, state-of-the-art lighting, and carefully selected furniture.

The Architecture of Place

Reed Kroloff

It helps to be a visionary if you want to imagine urban life in southern Arizona. Though beautiful, the Sonoran Desert argues powerfully against gathering large concentrations of people in it. This is not the soft, verdant landscape of the American dream. It is a jagged place, with spiny, leafless plants, constant sun, and an obdurate disinterest in accommodation.

And yet they come: architects planners, schemers and dreamers. Urban ecologist Paolo Soleri proposed massive, fantastically dense cities here, rising hundreds of stories into the air to minimize their footprints. Real estate developer Del Webb's Sun City, the first city-scale retirement community, went the opposite way: a vast, horizontal aggregation radiating out across the desert floor in concentric circles of new buildings and old flesh.

Webb's vision won, and despite the chaos it unleashed, for architects the desert still intoxicates, with its stark collision of beauty and challenge. Frank Lloyd Wright was the first modernist to understand it. He spoke reverently of the "dotted line" of the desert horizon and marveled at the structural characteristics of the saguaro cactus. He saw in this totalizing environment the chance to create a new and uniquely place-specific architecture. That impulse took form as Taliesin West, still the most important and influential work of contemporary architecture and urbanism in the American Southwest.

It continues today in the Phoenix Central Library, the monolithic masterpiece by Bruder/DWL Architects that is the first—and only—building to challenge Wright's, both intellectually and spiritually. Where Wright's compound hugs the ground over which it stretches, the Central Library stands upright, a great copper mesa sitting at the edge of Margaret T. Hance Park. Wright's building, all sticks and rocks and rippling fabric roofs, channeled a caravan headed west. The Central Library, by contrast, is a citadel, a reading redoubt, a refuge. Neither building looks nor feels like anything that came before it; they are *sui generis*.

In this way, Bruder connects directly to Wright (as well as indirectly, through Soleri, with whom he apprenticed; Soleri, in turn, apprenticed with Wright). He connects in other ways as well. Both Wright and Bruder are iconoclasts, lone wolves. Neither went to architecture school. Both exiled themselves to the edge of civilization to practice—Wright on a 700+ acre compound, miles beyond what was then the edge of Scottsdale, and Bruder to a smaller, more rustic ten-acre compound outside New River, at the northern-most perimeter of Greater Phoenix.

For Bruder, the kinship with Wright is occasionally aesthetic but mostly spiritual. In the work of both architects, regardless of location, invention reigns, interpretation guides, and themes emerge. Like Wright, Bruder enjoys abstraction. He makes mountains: from the plateau atop the Central Library to the craggy peaks of the Johnston Residence to the basalt chunk that is the Nevada Museum of Art. He makes canyons and fissures as well: see the Deer

Valley Petroglyph Preserve or, especially, the Byrne Residence. In the Nellis Cox Residence, he burrows; in the Townsend Residence, he perches. Many buildings have meandering pathways and landscapes that suggest rivers and eddies.

Nature is always close, but Bruder also celebrates technology. The Platt Residence, early in his career, offers an aesthetic nod to Wright with its raked-joint stone and concrete walls, but it is capped with a prefabricated space frame of his own invention. The Central Library's roof—which appears to float unsupported by either the building's columns or walls—is a dynamic essay in advanced cable-stay tectonics.

That roof also creates an opportunity for Bruder to deploy one of his most effective visual strategies—in the exquisitely narrow gap between the roof and the building's concrete walls. Light sheets down the vertical surfaces like water. Every cloud that passes overhead, every variation in the color of the sky, registers against the concrete in real time. When the light is at its brightest, the gap seems to swallow the edge of the roof itself, dematerializing it in the same way that artist James Turrell does in one of his skyspaces. The viewer is forced to question what they are seeing—or rather, perceiving—knowing full well that the edge is there, yet not certain where it ends and begins. It's a remarkable sensation.

The use of daylight has been central to Bruder's work from the beginning. He has experimented with coves, corners, reflective surfaces, textured surfaces, skylights, screens, shades, sails, and more. Certainly, this is at least in part a response to the particular conditions—and opportunities—of practice in a place where sun is the constant. It's no accident that Turrell's great masterwork, Roden Crater, is in the same state. Nor is it a surprise that Turrell called on Bruder to build two Turrell skyspaces in the Valley: *Knight Rise* at the Scottsdale Museum of Contemporary Art (also of Bruder's design) and *Air Apparent*, on the Arizona State University Tempe campus.

But for Bruder, light is about the phenomenological in architecture—the sensory, the kinetic, the remembered, the experienced. The subtitle of this book, "from head to heart to hand," neatly summarizes not only his creative process but his intent in the work: these buildings—with their artful control of light, texture, color, form, and craft—are designed to engage visitors viscerally.

A Bruder building is almost always candid about how it's made, how it interacts with a site, how it draws from local sources, how it wants you to act and feel in that place; in short, it's "Genius Loci." There is a drive in his work to make it so place-specific that it couldn't work anywhere else; he's the anti-Miesian. Try to imagine the outrageous texture and form of the Nellis Cox Residence somewhere other than the desert. It would make no sense.

At the same time, his architecture is unabashedly sculptural, textured, and often, seemingly still in process—very much in keeping with someone educated, as Bruder was, in late twentieth-century studio art (at the University of Wisconsin-Milwaukee). At the Hill Sheppard Residence, a jangling collision of articulated wedges climbing a central Phoenix hill, the mortar looks as if it isn't dry yet, still oozing out from between the concrete blocks. The Townsend Residence is slippery here and rough there as it negotiates its Paradise Valley site, a veritable constellation of circles and orbs—some metal, some concrete block masonry, some glass—that look as if they could rearrange themselves at any moment.

Bruder enjoys the dynamic of collisions, in both plan and elevation (see the Byrne Residence). Formally, he is drawn to wedges, blocks, and arcs, at times in combination, like in his New River studio or the Weiss Residence, and at times letting them stand clear, as at the Billings Public Library or the Sea Arc Residence. Similarly, his material choices owe as much to collage theory—articulation through juxtaposition—as they do to environmental or structural issues. As noted above, he is fascinated by technology, and his buildings reflect that visually: they often look like machines created for a particular site or challenge (like the Weiss Guys car washes or even Mad River Rafting).

Taken together, the body of work is compelling: dozens and dozens of individual residences, a handful of multifamily condominiums, offices, libraries, museums, and more. This book, divided between the years before and after Bruder completed a fellowship at the American Academy in Rome, holds only a sample. He has been building for more than fifty years now and is no longer the rangy recluse living in the back of beyond; he is even a fellow of the American Institute of Architects, an organization he spurned in his more radical days. Most surprisingly, he has left the desert and is now practicing in Portland, Oregon, a place and a climate that could not be more different from the one where he cut his architectural teeth. Then again, it is a place of relatively dense urbanism, more Arcology than Broadacre City.

Even without being in Phoenix, Bruder's influence endures, spreading well beyond his completed projects. Because, more than any other architect since Wright, Bruder is responsible for inspiring a new generation of modern architects that I dubbed the "Arizona School" in *Architecture* magazine some twenty years ago. In that issue, we identified about a dozen architects, practicing principally in Phoenix and Tucson, whose work was influenced directly by Bruder's (and Wright's). Several of them, including luminaries like Wendell Burnette and Rick Joy, had worked in Bruder's studio before founding their own practices. Today, that list has more than doubled and together they have created the critical mass necessary to counter the architectural and planning tsunami unleashed by Del Webb and others. This next generation (now two generations) has inherited the tradition pioneered by Wright and Bruder.

They are the next visionaries. But Bruder is far from gone: the Palm Tower, a 300-foot residential tower, will open in downtown Phoenix later this year. It's 500 floors shorter than Soleri might have imagined. But it's Bruder's first high-rise; give him time.

A Personal Take

Billie Tsien

I remember the first time I met Will—he walked in looking very much like a mountain man—long brown hair, brown beard, and the loping stride and powerful presence of a large man. He has always been a larger-than-life figure. Along with his outsized presence came an outsized generosity.

It was the 1990s and Tod Williams and I were in Phoenix to begin work on the Phoenix Art Museum—our first major commission. We were thrilled and also overwhelmed. Phoenix was much smaller then and you could still find orange groves where you could get fresh squeezed juice and date farms where you could get a date shake. There were still resorts where ladies in swim caps did water exercises in heart shaped swimming pools beneath the palm trees. Will, along with Wendell Burnette, was beginning his work on the Phoenix Central Library. Arriving from New York City, wearing our black city clothing and knowing little about the Southwest, Will was our guide to the desert.

He invited us up to visit him at his home in the desert. Driving up dusty roads that seemed to deteriorate the farther along we went—it was hard to imagine that anyone could inhabit this unforgiving landscape. Upon arrival—it didn't seem possible that Will could be living in what seemed to be a series of small wooden boxes. At the time, I remember them as being only slightly larger than a box that would contain some kind of appliance like a refrigerator. The boxes were connected by a wooden walkway. The buildings were so very modest—today we would say that they sit lightly on the land. And so, in his life and his work, Will revealed the hard beauty that is to be found in such a place. Looking at his projects was a lesson in making buildings that feel deeply a part of the land.

One night—on the eve of a presentation to a client for a house on the east coast—Will showed up at the studio in New York and asked if he could sit at a desk. Of course he was welcome. He proceeded to roll out paper and taped it down. Next came his drawing tools—this was a hand drawn presentation. He put his head down and began to work. The next morning when I can to the office, there was Will finishing up his drawings, having worked through the night. They were stunningly beautiful. And Will's smile that morning was also stunningly beautiful.

Will's positive energy glows incandescent and his optimism feels at times overwhelming. He pulls the work and those who work with him forward with the conviction of an absolute believer. And in the end we are all grateful he carried us along on his journey. Will has made powerful marks on the earth. He has created a body of work that sings of the dust and heat of the place where it was born.

A Rebel with a Cause

Robert McCarter

> "Radical though it be, the work here illustrated is dedicated to a cause conservative in the best sense of the word. At no point does it involve denial of the elemental law and order inherent in all great architecture; rather it is a declaration of love for the spirit of that law and order and a reverential recognition of the elements that made its ancient letter in its time vital and beautiful." —Frank Lloyd Wright, 1908

Will Bruder is a consummate architect. He can rightly be called an "architect's architect." This is because Bruder has consistently engaged with the pragmatic and poetic aspects of architecture, understanding that both are needed to construct an architecture that will conserve and enhance its place, that will enrich the experience of its inhabitants, that will contribute to the evolution of the discipline of architecture, and—most importantly—that will last. Though he never attended architecture school, throughout his long and remarkably productive career Bruder has always been the most diligent and dedicated "student" of the discipline of architecture—an architect who continually undertakes constructively critical analyses of the work of his historical predecessors and contemporary peers, incorporating the underlying ordering principles found there into his own work.

In the opening sentences of his essay "In the Cause of Architecture," which introduced the first national publication of his work, Frank Lloyd Wright characterizes his architecture as "radical," by which he meant an architecture that returns to beginnings, an architecture grounded in the foundational roots of the discipline. Bruder's work is often grouped with other architects whose works are directly or indirectly inspired by Wright's work, such as John Lautner and Bruce Goff, and while this is certainly not inappropriate, it also does not recognize and address Bruder's important contributions to the discipline of architecture. Rather than any similarity of forms, it is the rigorous engagement with the foundational ordering principles of architecture that connects the work of Will Bruder with that of Wright. Like Wright, Bruder is a self-taught architect, entering the profession through apprenticeship. Like Wright, Bruder has a small office that has been prolific in the construction of works of the highest quality over many years. Like Wright, Bruder has been an important mentor to the next generation of architects. Finally, like Wright, Bruder is a rebel with a cause—he works, as Wright did, "in the cause of architecture."

In addition to Wright, the list of modern American architects whose work Bruder has analyzed and learned from include Eero Saarinen, Bruce Goff, Paolo Soleri, and Gunnar Birkerts (the latter two with whom Bruder worked), among many others. The critically important time Bruder spent at the American Academy in Rome as the Rome Prize Fellow in 1987, occurring when he was forty years old, allowed him to analyze and learn from the work of modern European architects such as Carlo Scarpa, whose works are integrated into the historic and contemporary context of Venezia and the Veneto, and employ local material and construction traditions in a way that is unparalleled among modern practitioners. This experience in Rome, and the chance it provided Bruder to critically assess his work to date and recognize the disciplinary principles that underlie it, can be seen as a turning point in his career, reflected in the decision to organize this book into sections "before" and "after" his time at the American Academy. In addition, though at first glance it may seem unlikely —due to the seeming dissimilarity of the forms of their buildings—it can be argued that Bruder shares fundamental ethical, material, and constructive ordering principles with the modern American architect Louis I. Kahn.

Typical of Bruder's rigorous engagement with the discipline of architecture through analyses of historical and contemporary precedents is his "discovery," while working at Paolo Soleri's Cosanti studio in 1967, of the work of Paul Schweikher, as embodied in the Upton House in Scottsdale, Arizona, then in ruins after a fire. Due to his largely being absent from the standard histories of modern architecture, it is necessary to briefly introduce Schweikher here to understand his importance. Schweikher (1903-1997) worked in Illinois during the early years of his career, when he built his own remarkable house and studio outside Chicago in 1938. From 1953-56, he was head of Yale School of Architecture, during the time that Kahn was teaching there. In 1956 Schweikher was appointed head of Carnegie Architecture School in Pittsburgh, where he lived and worked for twelve years. In 1968 he retired from his teaching position, moved to Arizona, and continued to practice in the house and studio of his own design in Sedona. While apprenticing in Arizona, and before setting up his own practice in 1974, Bruder visited Schweikher's house in Sedona and met the architect, marking the start of a more than twenty-year relationship between the two men.

Bruder's analyses of Schweikher's work goes well beyond his similar studies of the works of other architects, and it has culminated in the forthcoming monograph *Paul Schweikher Architect*. One example of the constructive ways in which Bruder has engaged with Schweikher's work is his insightful analytical essay on the architect's own house and studio in Schaumburg, Illinois, of 1938 (with additions in 1948), which appears on the house's website. Schweikher's House and Studio is an altogether remarkable work that quite closely parallels Wright's first Usonian houses of the same time period, such as the Jacobs House of 1936 and the Pope House of 1939—as well as sharing intriguing parallels with Wright's own home and studio at Taliesin of 1911.

The Schweikher House and Studio is a one-story, horizontally extended structure, T-shaped in plan, with the three wings containing the living and dining rooms, the studio and cantilevered conference room, and the bedrooms and south-facing "solar dressing room," respectively, with the kitchen and entry breezeway at the intersection of the three wings. The house is constructed of interwoven wall planes of brick, set in a running bond, and board-and-batten redwood, with massive Douglas fir columns and beams, redwood wall and ceiling boards, and floor-to-ceiling glazing, as well as clerestory windows set beneath the cantilevered roof. The house is anchored by the massive fireplace, the slightly projecting hood of which is made of brick set in a vertical-end stack bond, which takes up the entire eastern wall of the living room.

This perhaps too-extensive introduction to the Schweikher House and Studio is necessary to provide context for the revealing parallels between Schweikher's work and that of Bruder. Among the insights Bruder makes in his essay on Schweikher's House and Studio—all of which could appropriately be applied to his own projects—he states: "The design for his own residence was driven by Schweikher's unique sense of scale and proportion, structural pragmatism, and passion for detail." In particular, Bruder's calling out of Schweikher's "structural pragmatism" in regard to the powerful way the massive brick walls and heavy wood columns and beams shape our experience of the space—the manner in which the poetic experience arises directly from the pragmatic construction—also characterizes Bruder's works.

Perhaps even more pertinent to understanding how Bruder draws lessons from the work of predecessors is his critical observation regarding a key spatial and experiential moment in the Schweikher House and Studio—the intersection of the solid brick wall on the living room's south side with the projecting brick fireplace hood on the east side of the room. He notes: "A vertical slot of daylight at the joint between wall and fireplace dramatically lightens the massive stack bond brick fireplace hood." It is precisely this use of thin, glazed slots of daylight to cut apart unlike materials and to articulate separate masses that is shared by Wright, in both his Prairie period and later works, by Kahn, most famously in his Salk Institute scientists' studies, and by Bruder.

Bruder's constructive engagement with the disciplinary history of architecture centers on the pragmatic and the poetic, place and climate, and on the material shaping of experience. His works epitomize the contemporary evolution of what Kenneth Frampton has called the "tectonic culture" of architecture—the history of architecture understood not as having to do with the formal concerns of the historian, but rather with the poetics of construction and the matters of making with which architecture as a métier is inextricably intertwined in its practice in the lifeworld. Bruder's conception of architecture may be said to return to the discipline's ancient roots in the poetics of construction, as is evidenced by his "intensive reading" of the works of E. E. Viollet-le-Duc while designing the Phoenix Central Library.

In his writings, dating from the 1850s, Viollet-le-Duc proposed an interpretation of architectural history, and a form-language of design, both of which were determined and inspired by the necessities of construction, with particular emphasis on structure—including his proposals for astonishing (yet tectonically logical) hybrid structures of iron and masonry. Viollet-le-Duc's writings and design examples are paralleled by the work of his colleague Henri Labrouste, in particular his Bibliothèque Nationale, begun in 1854, with its grid of cast-iron columns supporting arched wrought-iron trusses, which in turn carry the nine ceramic masonry tile domes of the ceiling, each with a circular skylight at its center. It is no coincidence that Bruder includes a photograph of the interior of Labrouste's Bibliothèque Nationale in his presentation of the Phoenix Central Library.

The top-level reading room of Bruder's library—one of the truly great rooms of our time—involves a remarkable transposition of Labrouste's ceramic, sky-lit domes, each supported by four cast-iron columns, into Bruder's circular skylights set directly above the concrete columns carrying the astonishing tensegrity cable-net structure that supports the slightly curving plane of the hovering roof. While the Phoenix Central Library received the AIA's

Twenty-five Year Award, the highest honor given for a building, it's worth noting the unusually large number of branch libraries among Bruder's works, this in a time when the library as an institution is put ever more into question. But Bruder clearly believes that while libraries will need to evolve, they will remain a key cultural institution for establishing the public realm and centering community life.

In Bruder's works, materials are engaged with the intention of bringing out their space-shaping character and experience-engendering quality. While this is accomplished through often entirely unexpected detailing, it is always done with precise intention with respect to the activities of the inhabitants. Bruder's works are characterized by the play between the lightweight framing of the tectonic overhead and the earthbound masses of the stereotomic, and we often find solid masses being sliced open by lines of light, and slices of light separating and articulating elements and volumes. Bruder's work is the result of a design process that begins by taking things apart, analyzing them for their core characteristics, and then putting them back together again, reassembling them in the most logical yet often unexpected way, usually with open joints between, in ways that emphasize both the independence and interdependence of space-shaping planes—a way of working shared by architects as diverse as Gerrit Rietveld, Wright, and Kahn. While the materials and forms Bruder employs can often be seen as paralleling the work of Wright, particularly in their connection to and responsiveness to place, the way Bruder assembles forms and spaces and composes plans parallels the work of Kahn. Like Kahn and Wright, Bruder is inspired by the way vernacular and indigenous architecture is adapted to and shaped by its place, its climate, its material, and its light. Like Wright and Kahn—and Scarpa—Bruder is primarily concerned with how to put things together in order to make buildings, the experience of which is characterized by the marks of their making.

I would like to conclude by suggesting that, in addition to these architectural qualities shared by Bruder's work with that of Wright and Kahn, there is another, equally important, parallel. As Wright and Kahn's work did in their respective times, so Bruder's work stands in opposition to the contemporary tendency of the architectural profession to be increasingly dominated by the pursuit of a universal self-generating formalism, disengaged from regional material culture, landform, climate, and the particular qualities of place, and emphasizing exterior form-making over experiential place-making. The design process for these uniformly interpreted design formulas involves predetermined formal parameters being applied without regard to the qualities of context, climate, and program, and the materials out of which they are made have little to no effect on their design. On the other hand, the design process shared by Wright, Kahn, and Bruder is concerned with doing what fits into preexisting conditions and what is appropriate as regards the qualities of material, context, climate, and program. Above and beyond its exceptional spatial and experiential richness, what makes Will Bruder's work worth studying is that it results from a process of design where the architect seeks a fit between function and form, fitting the spatial geometry to the pattern of human activity, and where the materials with which a building is made have a significant effect on its experience.

Crafting Place, Building Legacy: Will Bruder's Enduring Impact

Teresa Rosano

Standing on stage, with long untamed hair, an even longer beard, and dressed in casual corduroy and denim—an anomaly in the profession—Will Bruder was unlike any other architect to appear in the University of Arizona, College of Architecture lecture hall. He wasn't clad all in black, sporting pretentious spectacles. Will was larger than life, with a countercultural disregard for convention, and he appeared comfortable to be just that. He was relaxed and ready for the room overflowing with students. My classmates and I arrived to standing room only. Shoulder to shoulder, we waited curiously to see what the room's excitement was about.

I had already been in the presence of his work. My classmates and I had, by then, regularly trespassed onto one of his projects under construction near the university. It was a rare opportunity to see truly innovative design and construction happening just minutes from campus. But that Friday marked my first chance to listen to the ideas behind the concrete, steel, and wood we had been visiting. It was also the first time I heard a passionate plea for architecture, its power to embody a mission to make change in the world.

Will's way of speaking is unparalleled—part preacher, part teacher. He has a warm, conviction-filled voice. His agenda that afternoon was clear: to reveal the behind-the-scenes strategy that won him the commission for the Phoenix Central Library. In dramatic fashion, each pause building anticipation, he recounted how he placed a jewel-like object into an expansive model of downtown Phoenix, as if presenting it once more to the jury. At the time, we couldn't fully grasp the significance of what we were witnessing, but it was clear that Will wasn't just an architect—he was a storyteller, an optimistic visionary. That moment felt pivotal in his journey, even if we didn't fully understand its meaning at the time.

As I continued to follow his work in the years that followed, it became increasingly clear that Will Bruder wasn't interested in architecture for architecture's sake. He saw it as something much larger—a means of shaping lives and the world.

His use of materials—like a sculptor allowing the rawness of concrete, steel, and wood to tell their own stories—resonated with me immediately. It reflected a desert value: rugged, unpolished, but beautiful in its authenticity. The desert, in its rawness, spoke through his work, and this became a guiding principle in our firm's design philosophy.

As he orchestrates curves and angles, light and shadow, with a playful wit, it's clear that Will understands a place—whether it's the desert or another context—on a level that makes each site come to life.

Nearly ten years later, I again recognized Will's impact. Several Arizona architects, including my partner, Luis Ibarra and I, gathered in a parking lot near Phoenix for a group photoshoot. This time, Bruder was dressed all in black—perhaps because the instructions had advised against it. We were part of what would become known as the "Arizona School," a group of architects selected by Reed Kroloff for his outgoing farewell issue of *Architecture Magazine*. As the youngest members of that cohort and from Tucson, Luis and I were unfamiliar to the rest. As we packed into vans to go even deeper into the desert, we were asked who we were, where we had come from. Most of the others had worked in Will Bruder's office at some point. The interwoven stories they shared on the dusty ride to the Superstition Mountains revealed just how far his influence reached. It was as if he was the architectural Godfather of the Arizona School, a legacy passed down from Paolo Soleri and Frank Lloyd Wright but imbued with his own experimental spirit. Will's ability to find the extraordinary in the ordinary, to extract beauty from the rawness of the desert, was something we were all fortunate to inherit.

For Luis and me, Will's mentorship came not in the form of structured guidance but as remote encouragement. The first time we met him, we were elated that he was even aware of us and our work. To be noticed by someone like him was affirming—he saw something in us and encouraged us to see more in ourselves. Over the years, his kindness and generosity continued, as he consistently praised our work and pushed us to trust our instincts. A key lesson in his advice: don't give up, stick to what you believe, believe in architecture.

His style is unique. Unlike Soleri or Wright, Will's approach is more spatially and materially experimental, especially in his residential projects. Each house he designs is as unique as its site and the people who live there. He doesn't impose a vision; instead, he sees each project anew, capturing the essence of a place and translating it into architecture. His ability to adapt and respond to both environment and human experience sets him apart. It's this openness, this willingness to experiment again and again, that makes his work not only innovative but deeply personal.

It wasn't until another decade and a half later that I fully grasped Will's profound devotion to architecture as a lifelong practice. When our firm was shortlisted for Tucson's January 8th Memorial competition, we needed a critical eye. Luis called Will, and he promptly invited us to his office. The next day, we packed up our entire team and headed to Phoenix.

Will spent hours with us, listening intently, poring over our ideas, and getting excited with every detail. He brainstormed how to refine the design, what materials to consider, and what perspectives we needed to explore. He saw the potential immediately and generously offered his resources, even calling in his team of artists and artisans to assist us. "You've got something important to create," he said, "we need to mobilize everything we can."

Will wasn't just a passive observer; he invested himself in the success of our vision. It wasn't about ownership of the idea—it was about the faithful pursuit of the best one, a philosophy that resonates deeply with him. For weeks, he sent suggestions, checked in regularly, and even drove down to Tucson with two international architects to attend our public presentation.

When the project ultimately went to another firm, calling Will to break the news was one of the hardest things I've ever had to do. His disappointment seemed to exceed our own —not in us, but in the lost opportunity to bring a meaningful idea to life.

This is the essence of Will Bruder: a master architect who sees his role as more than just building structures. He builds possibilities. His belief in the power of architecture is not a lofty ideal—it's a living, breathing practice. In a profession often swayed by commercial pressures or convention, Will remains steadfast in his belief in the transformative potential of architecture.

His legacy endures not only in the remarkable buildings he's designed but also in the architects he's inspired and mentored. Will Bruder's passionate reverence for architecture and his commitment to design as a life's practice are rare. He has shown us all that architecture, at its best, can truly make a difference in the world—and from my perspective, he has.

Chasing Architecture

J. Meejin Yoon and Eric Höweler

Chasing architecture with Will Bruder across the Louisiana bayou was an experience both nerve racking (we have never driven so fast) and nourishing (we had never taken so much in). We had just met Will at a conference organized by the Louisiana AIA chapter where we had taken turns on stage to present our work. We of course knew of Will and his precedent-setting architecture prior to our back-to-back talks in Louisiana. His design for the Phoenix Public Library was a landmark building not only in Phoenix but in the discipline—a masterfully executed manifesto on desert regionalism. Hearing Will share the story of competing for the library and his uncompromising stance on the design principles throughout the process was inspiring and daunting all at once. Spending two days with him at the conference, he was gracious with his time and generous with his conversation, and he proposed driving back to New Orleans and seeing architecture along the way. Will wanted to see a particular work of architecture just outside of Baton Rouge...and so we set off across the bayou in two cars. We raced to keep up with him to make it in time before the sunset. When we got there, the attendant stated that the facility was closed for renovations and was thus inaccessible to the public. However, Will would not be deterred. With his persistent and impassioned explanation for our architectural pilgrimage, the facilities director relented and gave us permission to enter the structure. No sooner were we in the first space than we found Will supine on his back, looking under a skylight to figure out how it was made and how it worked. I remember thinking to myself, this is a world-famous architect but he is sprawled on the floor sketching and taking note of a detail. Will is that kind of architect. For Will, the lessons were in the building itself, around every corner, and in every detail.

Will would become not only a mentor and role model but a coach and a champion. Getting to know him over the next few years, we learned how he had built his successful practice. He was working all over the world on enviable commissions but despite the scale and growth of the practice, he felt a need to return to his core principles of architecture. He took the dramatic step of leaving his own accomplished practice, built over many decades, in order to relaunch a practice on his own terms that reflected the values he held most dear. This dramatic move was astounding to us. How could one leave one's own practice to start anew? But it makes total sense for Will, an architect whose integrity and commitment to practicing architecture on his own terms is a constant reminder of an architect's agency in the practices they build. For Will, architecture and life are so intertwined and the design of the practice is a design project in and of itself. For Will, architecture practice needs nurturing, care, and maintenance but also a committed determination to practice on one's own terms.

Before meeting Will in Louisiana, we had studied his work and visited the Phoenix Public Library several times. The building's massiveness, gently bowed but rugged copper clad structure, presented a rather mute face to the surrounding context. By entering the building, one finds a world within, one that is surprisingly light filled and material rich. Studying the plan we discerned that the buildings north-south orientation is designed to shield the building from the low angle east and west sun. The glazing is reserved for the north and south facades where they are carefully protected by exterior sunshades and skylights bring dramatic light into the reading room. The articulation of the structure in the reading room consisting of columns supporting cable trusses that support the roof but stop short of the surface allows the circular skylights to focus light on the tops of the columns and highlight the unique and original detail. This single detail is deserving of a whole book. Will gave this detail intense attention, and incredible thought and care went into it to make it an extraordinary architectural treatise. Will takes the constraints of climate and context and turns it into an alchemy for extraordinary moments of architecture.

Architecture is deep in Will's DNA. He can't hold it back...and, when you see a twinkle in his eye and his stride gets longer, before you know it he is ten feet ahead of you as he accelerates toward an object of his architectural curiosity. All you can do is try to keep up. And while it is impossible to keep up with superhuman stride, in trying to, one learns how to be a better architect. Will's contagious enthusiasm and ethical north star continue to inspire generations of architects. We feel privileged to have chased him through the bayou and have been following him ever since.

Bruder's America & The Invention of a Laminar Tectonic

Nader Tehrani

Prologue

The Phoenix Central Library opened its doors in 1995, but for the young practitioner that I was, the building also opened my eyes to a unique condition that defined American architecture in its time. By way of context, the decade before that had seen a construction boom, with the rise of corporate architecture under the inertia of postmodernism, and this, in turn, had given materiality to a new way of building. After the waning days of Brutalism, with the barren materiality of concrete, wood, and glass on their way out, architecture was revisiting the glory of Bramante, Palladio, and Alberti through the eyes of figures like Michael Graves, James Stirling, and Robert Venturi whose translation of classicism was not only mediated by their education in modernism, but even more so by the standardized construction systems of their time. Under this new regime, the deep poché of load-bearing walls would be entrusted to the pitiful frailty of a 2 × 4 stud wall with a 5⁄8" Sheetrock veneer. That is not to say that these same buildings did not enjoy the splendor of weighty granites and opulent marbles, but what they all somehow lacked was a strategy to translate these new laminar systems of construction into contemporary terms. By extension, the debates of academia were primarily couched in either theoretical terms, borrowing from philosophy, semiotics, and other fields, or were materialized primarily in pictorial terms, escaping construction as a productive terrain for debate. Through the clarity of its constructed systems, the Phoenix Central Library captured both a physical and discursive quality that was virtually absent in the architecture of its time—what I will try to expand on in this brief essay.

The Curious Mind

One day in late 1995, I received a call on a landline—the only type common at the time—from a gentleman who introduced himself as Will Bruder. Having already seen the Phoenix Library in *Architect Magazine*, I was familiar with the name, but also street-smart enough to know the call was a prank to which I would play along.

Enthusiastically, the caller launched into an analysis of Casa La Roca—our recently premiated project in Progressive Architecture[1] —an analysis of such detail that it would have defied the abilities of just any prankster, thus narrowing down my list of culprits; I knew I was at least speaking to an architect. It was only later in his filibuster of praise, when the gentleman would divulge the details of jury comments, that I started to mistrust my intuition, realizing I had been duped: not by an imposter but by the one and only Will Bruder, who had passionately led the jury to its results. He would fly to Boston a few weeks later and pay a visit to our office, where he would display the curiosity, patience, and enthusiasm that are a deep-seated part of his character.

An Alternative Pedagogy

Free from the shackles of a conventional architectural pedagogy, Bruder was educated as an artist. Others will elaborate more faithfully on the tutelage of Paolo Soleri and Gunnar Birkerts, but his entry into architecture revolved around direct engagement and practice—an empirical process. On the one hand, as a sculptor, Bruder relished material properties as much as he enjoyed his collaborations with the trades whose knowledge of means and methods would often inform his moments of invention. On the other hand, trained through

1 The Progressive Architecture Awards were the one and only significant awards program for unbuilt architecture. Premised on actual commissions, the idea of the awards series was to celebrate speculative and experimental work of its time.

practice, he would educate himself through direct experience of spaces, places, and what he came to appreciate as architectural phenomena. Indeed, his appreciation of the world, its cultures and histories, all primarily stem from his myriad visits to architectural sites—pilgrimages that were visually far more detailed than any architectural book could cover.

In effect, if conventional students were educated by standards of professionalism, then they were also tested by two poles of cultural legitimation. They were expected to know the architectural canons and to weigh in on a historical body of work that, in some way, had been preordained, with authority. But they were also trained to become part of a professional workforce, to know construction conventions, and to work with industry standards. Bruder's less-than-orthodox entry into the discipline freed him from the very limitations that the canons would have cast on him from above and the industry would have prepackaged for him from below.

A Different Era from the Modern Masters

Bruder's own position within history is no less relevant to this argument: long gone were the days of grand patronage and the assumed authority of the architect as a centralized figure. For the most part, mid-century figures such as Eero Saarinen, Gordon Bunshaft, and Paul Rudolf saw the end of their careers by the 1960s and '70s. With their departure, and a new eye on corporate protocols, there emerged a form of institutional standardization that aligned effectively with the rampant expansion of the American suburbs—a world that Bruder would inherit. No longer was "standardization" a modernist polemic, but a burden of American conventionalism and acquiescence to industry practices, something Bruder would have to work hard on to overturn. Bruder may have viewed the promise of architecture from the extraordinary achievements of these predecessors, but his immediate obstacles came in the form of practices that would almost entirely obliterate the possibility of the architectural imagination he had cultivated.

Embedded within Means and Methods

Bruder's early years of practice in Arizona opened up avenues for modest forms of local patronage: first, houses of moderate size, and later, institutional projects with a civic imagination. Notwithstanding, these commissions operated with relatively modest budgets that required a genuine understanding of conventional building practices --what Bruder would navigate towards bespoke details and well-crafted materials. Unlike his predecessors, Bruder also had to collaborate with and mediate between complex stakeholder groups, participatory design processes, and intensive engagement with communities. If control of architectural vision is one of the ultimate myths that education cultivates, then Bruder had to work against the grain of that narrative to build trust through material knowledge and a process of inclusion that, in an uncanny way, gave him even more control over the specifications he required.

Long before the days of Home Depot, Bruder would work from the materiality of the commonplace to forge a connection with builders whose familiarity with construction systems was grounded in conventional practices. One could say that instead of resisting the "ordinary," Bruder operated as a Trojan Horse, communicating with builders through a kit of parts they recognized as wholly part of their own lexicon. Bruder's understanding of the trades—and their means and methods—become a strategic *leitmotif* of his practice, overturning convention through the seduction of extraordinary crafts, allowing the trades to see areas of invention embedded in their own work, hitherto untapped. He often worked with their details, practices, and sense of economies as a launching pad, but invariably he also deformed, transformed, and deviated in ways that defamiliarized the reality of the everyday, something that came to radicalize his buildings.

The Rational Configuration, the Speculative Figure

As planner, Bruder operates as a deep-seated rationalist, with building layouts that are beguilingly simple in their configurational and typological affinities. Deformations in these plans commonly emerge as a result of adaptions to topography, sun orientation, exceptional views, or other such environmental phenomena. With an appreciation of Alvar Aalto and Carlo Scarpa as backdrop, one can revisit Bruder's plans in order to examine how he would interpret, and subsequently transform their thinking: with Aalto, it was the way in which an organic "figure" is introduced onto a rationalist armature, and with Scarpa, the way in which sequential experiential phenomena become alibis for planning strategies that evade preconceived orders, be they symmetrical or serial. Absent of the city as a cultural reference point, Bruder often works with the natural landscape as a source for both spatial and semantic orientation; for him, mesas, canyons, and saguaros are not only natural elements but come with an architectural potency ripe for translation.

Bruder manages to reconcile two distinct architectural tendencies, the first dictating strong *partis*, diagrams, and organizational tropes, and the second allowing for open-ended spatial research, flexible planning, and a diagram that invites metabolic expansion when required. Thus, Bruder's buildings come from a place that is deeply practical in their programmatic responsibilities, but also equally compositionally speculative in terms of spatial and organizational adaption. Still, in my mind, what manifests as the most salient aspect of his architecture is how his planning is manifest through its material conditions: specifically, the way in which Bruder thinks through the detail, a priori, as a catalyst for his transfiguration of conventions into extraordinary architectural conditions, moments of invention, and episodes of experiential epiphany.

The Tectonic Mind: The Catalytic Detail

If the architecture of the 1980s was characterized by the expansive mindset of evoking other histories, it often lacked an intellectual project for "tectonic" thinking—treating construction akin to a pictorial practice. Whether in the articulation of thick, load-bearing walls, or in the thinness of light, diaphanous surfaces, the conventional tool kit of details often relegated architects to industry standards whose 2 × 6 Kawneer window frames, brick veneered curtain walls, and hollow stud-walled interiors were composed as a stage set for visual desires, almost entirely evacuated from tectonic nuance.

Thus, an invigorated discussion on tectonics is at the core of this argument. Construed in divergent ways, some theorists have commonly constructed an alliance between constructive thinking and a morality of truth, with the "honesty" of materials, functions, and building performance as evidence. Other theorists have oriented tectonics around the question of representation, and how architectural language serves as the medium through which expression is gauged. Bruder's work cuts through this dichotomy—one could say a false one—to explore how tectonic assemblies absorb and negotiate between material actualities with linguistic imaginations, programmatic functions and expressive projections, technical performance and visual theatricality.

From a methodological perspective, the primacy of materials and their requisite means of assembly form a more important part of the imaginative process for Bruder than an open-ended drawing process. In this sense, while his loose sketches are a delight to behold, they often conceal the constructive precision behind his thinking, what is normatively happening on a parallel track, at a different scale. For instance, as he scales up the drawing of a wall, the plane that he represents on paper is not merely an abstraction but rather a constructed entity; Bruder constructs the drawing as a prerequisite for "building." He doesn't merely draw lines but stacks them as if laying masonry. I am reminded of Louis I. Kahn's First Unitarian Church of Rochester, New York, and of how, in the absence of the ability to build with actual thickness, he would plan the exterior wall with chapel-like bays, producing the illusion of depth with what was only a brick veneer construction system. If Kahn evoked the weight of "the Ancients" through this spatial device, he also achieved it through tectonic dexterity, in contrast to the blunt pictorial bias of the architecture of the 1980s. The denial of material agency that was characteristic of that era, Bruder overturns, underscoring the instrumentality of building matter as the prerequisite for architectural action.

Thickness: Assembled Stereotomy

From a lineage that includes such characters as Sigurd Lewerentz, Kahn, and Wright, Bruder builds a narrative all his own, examining dimensions of materials, building systems, and conventional means of assembly. Through this, he arrives at an understanding less dependent on preconceived architectural forms, and more aligned with a construction process that biases material units, the labor of assembly, and the crafted detail as the basis of value. Consider the age-old example of the Doric column and its requisite entasis. The classical column was conceived and delivered through a combination of protocols: the carving of blocks that are of a size that can be lifted into position, the stacking of those blocks as cylinders, the chiseling of fluting that gives vertical continuity to what is fundamentally a stacked system, and most importantly, the sculpting of the column to render its entasis, which bears the evidence of weight as its expression. That last step delves into the realm where the effects rendered onto the column serve as a surplus to mere necessity, and this is where Bruder's internalization of tectonic culture allows him to examine thickness, thinness, weight, and lightness with phenomenological nuance.

There is possibly nothing more mundane than the 8 × 16 concrete block in contemporary construction, and for that very reason, it is most often used as the inner core of composite walls—or, alternatively, as infill between the structure of industrial sheds. For Bruder, this economic block would become a source of exploration and experimentation, squeezing depth, texture, and figuration out of a humble medium. Conventional wisdom and construction tolerances call for a wall to be erected in such a fashion—to demonstrate a level, plumb, and right relationship of parts to whole. For his Temple Kol Ami, Bruder misaligns the blocks in limited dimensions such that they maintain structural integrity, while using the severity of the Arizona sun to capture the depth of every misalignment, allusively evoking the image of Jerusalem's Western Wall. Semantically, maybe what is more important about this reference than its cultural quotation is that the displacement of blocks produces the sensation of archaic construction: Bruder displaces the idea of the image by the perceptual qualities of sensation, and the mere offset of a ¼ inch allows the mind to read blocks akin to four-feet deep. In effect, the imperfection of this wall's alignments leads to the perfection of a particular architectural experience.

Similarly, for the Hill Sheppard Residence, Bruder draws lessons from Lewerentz: not so much focused on the concrete block itself but more so on the mortar, the space between. If the labor of setting masonry involves the laying down of mortar, followed by the insertion of a block, and the swiping clean of mortar edges, then Bruder eradicates the third step from the mason's expected practice. A texture is born out of the imperfection of seeping mortar, the organization of the running bond giving visual cadence to the disarray of mortar overflow.

For the Nellis Cox Residence, Bruder plays on the innate craft of "clinker" bricks but taps into the inner structure of the concrete block as its basis; that is, the double-H configuration that produces its hollow interior. Broken into halves and rotated on edge, the blocks are laid out to produce the rustication of its courtyard wall. Capturing light in all the serendipitous ways possible, the character of this space emerges not so much from the perfection of the smooth concrete block as conceived for the market, but rather from an inner constitution whose structure gives discipline to the imperfections of its grotto-esque surface. If the artful craft of these textures plays on the accidental nature of the laborer's hand, the precision of the configurational thinking is not lost on Bruder.

So too, in the stacked corbeled wall of the Byrne Residence we discover a deliberate exactitude that is present throughout he entire body of Bruder's work, with the wall leaning away from the house to open a crack above, allowing the light to illuminate the texture of the wall in its inescapable perfection. The concrete block, perfunctory in its aesthetic promise as it may seem to the untrained eye, is transformed into a myriad of effects by a simple dimensional offset.

As individual commissions, these projects address their own programs, challenges, and problems. However, what binds them together is an intellectual project rooted in the material transformation of a single medium, transported from one commission to the next, with an eye towards the production of knowledge—what I am attempting to characterize as the unique promise of this work as a whole.

Thinness: The Laminar Industry

If Temple Kol Ami's main hall is defined by blocks that envelope the space of prayer, then the wings that extend classrooms towards the south expose the end-grain of the same blocks on the southern flank, revealing the precarity of the block as a tectonic unit. The tectonic effect associated with this thinness is confronted not as liability but as an experiential asset —something that Bruder explores with some consistency.

Averse to denial, much of the work is dedicated to finding a strategic expression for the reality of laminar construction as we know it today—be it with plywood, Sheetrock, polycarbonate panels, or even concrete block walls. For this reason, the tectonic effect produced by the slanted wall of the Byrne Residence is even more poignant, creating out of a compressive system of aggregation the effects of a wall in tension. Accordingly, when Bruder adopts Cor-Ten steel walls for the Deer Valley Petroglyph Preserve, the razor-like thinness of the steel walls appears natural; the "honesty" of its laminar extrusion is only exacerbated by the thinness he exposes on the edges of walls and canopies. This is only enhanced further as one witnesses the tilt-up concrete panels whose smooth edges serve as a foil for the thick geological amalgamations of aggregate fragments on its raw side (the result of copper slag in the bottom of formwork).

Thinness is not so much a choice but an imperative of this historic moment. What is a choice is the denial of its existence, to which Bruder spends an inordinate time artfully crafting a series of responses that accept the reality of our era but raise the stakes of thinness to a poetic edge. For this reason, it is maybe no surprise when we see the systemic frontal address to the laminar thinness of our contemporary condition in the Agave Branch Library. Here, within what would otherwise be construed as a generic "big box," the lyrical transformations of sheet materials are exploited in their many iterations, with stacked bond walls whose crenellated tops frame the sky beyond, padded quilted walls that serve as acoustic mitigation, chromatic polycarbonate walls that produce immersive translucent interiors, and simple steel tablets that frame the book shelves; all of these together create a language for contemporary technologies for which no others have developed an apt expression.

From Material Facts to Transcendence

Maybe the most beguiling aspect of Bruder's work stems from the directness of his material resources and the corollary indirectness of their requisite effects. The apparent contradiction behind his clinical protocols in combination with transcendent effects produces a consistent wonder that only experience can capture. What photography captures eloquently in the oeuvre almost never matches the necessity of spatial immersion within the architectural promenades Bruder choreographs in great detail, a movement that is cinematic in its splendor and attention to the fourth dimension. The light that is anticipated, the views that are framed, the sense of levity and weight, none of these can aptly be captured outside of direct experience.

It is with this sense of estrangement that I have returned to Bruder's buildings each time, awaiting new discoveries on each visit. Of them all, the Phoenix Central Library delivers repeatedly. The irrepressible relationship between structure, light, and weight is delivered with such mastery that one can almost never ascend to the reading room without a sense of awe. The synthetic triangulation between these three architectural strategies would suggest a conventional integration that the solution defies. Indeed, the self-conscious alignment of columns with skylights overhead produces the impossibility of structural trabeation. Thus, the necessity of structural displacement introduces the tensegrity as alibi to stretch the vectoral forces towards the saddlebags on the east and west. The roof, then, is laid down as a thin membrane, falling short of its supporting walls, capturing a crack of light that illuminates the walls. In turn, the walls are punctuated by a cadence of oculi, receiving the structure's tensile members before disappearing into a void: a lacuna escaping our visual reach but also our desire for rational reconciliation. The moment of wonder, then, is reserved for the delicate moment of levity, as the skylights hover inexplicably over the supporting columns, a roof pulled down as much as held up. It is this sensation that defies conventional logic, what becomes for Bruder a *leitmotif* for constant invention.

A real architect must...

Be both a poet and a pragmatist.

Be a leader, not a survivor!

Be insatiably curious and without complacency.

Always remember that architecture happens because of the client, not in spite of the client.

Learn from the past, but live in the future.

Never ignore the power of 'place' – both natural and manmade.

Be humble enough to realize perfection is impossible, but arrogant enough to keep reaching for it!

Possess an integrity to focus, complemented by an ability to laugh!

Be both passionate and compassionate.

Be a great listener and enjoy the music of life!

from a Keynote Address to the American Institute of Architectural Students Fall Forum, November 25, 1993

post Rome projects: 1986-2025

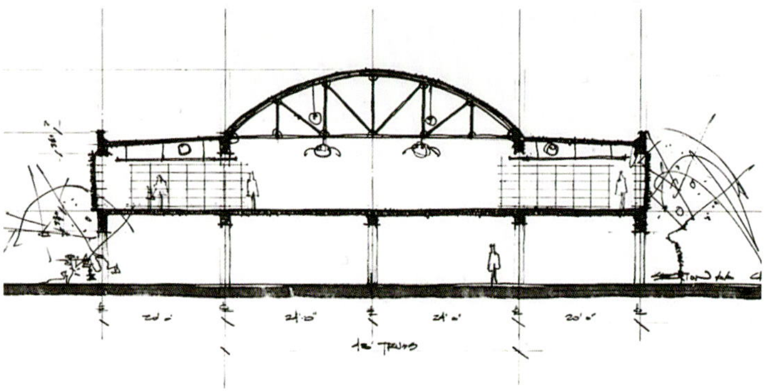

phoenix public library

Cholla Branch Library

Phoenix, Arizona, 1986

The site for the Cholla Branch of the City of Phoenix Library system included an existing twenty-year-old 10,000-square-foot branch library, once one of the busiest branch libraries in the country. An extremely successful city library policy had placed branch libraries within major shopping malls, thus increasing and overlapping activities in high-frequency use areas. The public then approved a bond issue to transform the Cholla branch into a 30,000-square-foot regional branch.

The architecture shows respect for and understanding of Phoenix's original late nineteenth-century, settler-built architecture: masonry and metal buildings that met the challenges of the desert climate and scant resources. The library is a commonsense expression of "zero maintenance" materials sculpted into a two-story beacon at the edge of a parking lot. The exterior material palette is composed of three materials: sandblasted cast-in-place concrete, galvanized metal with natural finish, and glass. These materials are maintenance-free and weather with dignity in the harsh Arizona sun. The galvanized metal siding shimmers like a mirage in the heat of the day, only to cool at dusk and reflect the night.

Entry is across an outdoor plaza that offers shaded seating and native desert landscaping. The "Cholla Corral" is fenced by a "squiggle-form" undulating, perforated galvanized metal wall.

The exterior envelops an inward-focusing environment like that of the adjacent shopping mall. Held within the original structure are new books, fiction, and juvenile and children's collections.

No attempt is made to disguise the past. A concrete drum containing the newly added children's area softens the building's presence on the street. A continuous slot through the concrete barrel's base is calibrated to be at children's height, offering them a live view of "outside" while "inside," as do the books.

A grand staircase at the center of the plan leads to a vaulted reading room spanned by exposed custom steel trusses. Lighting is suspended on aircraft cable.

Photos: © Tim Hursley, unless indicated

adult non-fiction
magazines and newspapers

information
adult non-fiction

You are now on final approach to Biddulphland
NOW PONTIAC, TOO

Weiss Guys Car Wash
Glendale, Arizona, 1987

Upon return from his six-month Rome Prize Travel and Study Grant in the fall of 1987, Bruder's first new commission was to design a new "ground-up" Weiss Guys Car Wash facility. Prior to this opportunity, he had completed a dynamic triangular cantilevered home on the west face of Mummy Mountain in Paradise Valley for Jerry and Elaine Weiss and their family. In addition, Bruder's renovations of several of their other car washes had been eye-catchingly well received!

While simple in its functional program and extremely modest in budget, this endeavor had to visually stand out from its site's nondescript frontage along a well-traveled east-west traffic artery. It was to be located beneath a totally overscaled advertising billboard, which had to be maintained for financial income reasons.

Thus, after defining the site's perimeter with simple, horizontally striated walls of sandblasted concrete blocks of various aggregates, the architecture takes the form of three dramatically simple exposed weathered steel cantilevered beam assemblies as they serve to support three thin-rolled galvanized box rib vaults for shade protection from the intense Arizona sun. Gas pumps, prewash vacuuming, and the wash tunnel equipment are all artfully protected.

Customers enter the retail waiting area under a circular metal canopy where they can watch, through generous glazing, their cars being washed while they shop for car-related merchandise. On exit, a clutch of landscaping softens the transition from indoor to outdoor, offering a breath of freshness before customers hit the road again in their sparkling clean cars.

Photos: © Scot Zimmerman

Nellis Cox Residence

Cave Creek, Arizona, 1987

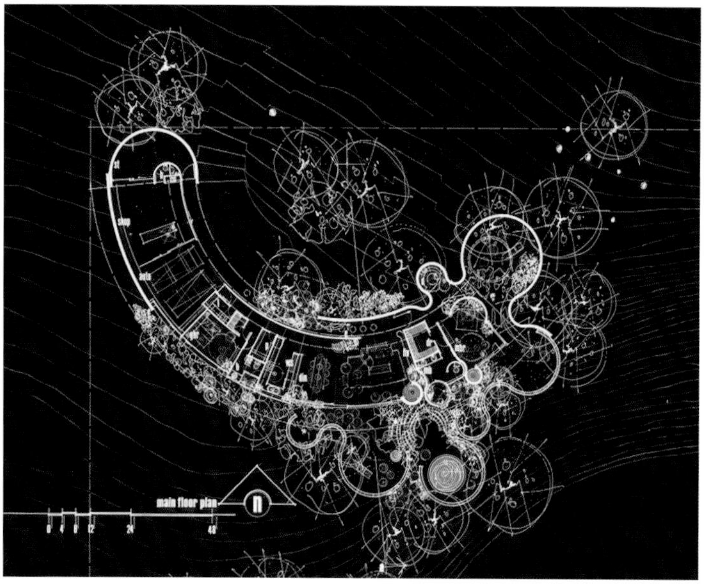

This earth-integrated residence is a passive solar solution to indoor/outdoor desert living. Designed for a couple who aspired to a natural "stone house," the inventive use of more affordable broken concrete block, rescued from deposits in an area landfill, became the distinctive materiality of this simple, crescent-shaped, shed-roofed house. With one organizing center point, the arc-shaped plan creates privacy and diversity of views, as it captures both morning and afternoon light. Radially organized, inside and out, the random rough textures and variegated colors and aggregates of the sandblasted block walls stand in contrast to polished concrete floors, magically minimal transparent glazing, and the warm wood finish of walls, ceiling, and cabinets. Primitive yet refined, the broken block house is a playful retreat in which to discover the desert it inhabits.

Photos: © Timothy Hursley

Murray Residence

New River, Arizona, 1988

Designed as a retirement residence for two former Phoenix public schoolteachers with a lifelong aspiration of living in the desert in an architecturally inspiring house, this modest 2,340-square-foot home is a study in processional movement and optimally framed desert views. Set carefully on a five-acre site, it is constructed of exposed polychrome, sandblasted concrete masonry block walls that appear to extend out from the natural landscape. Facing southeast, a low-pitched gable is set on the masonry walls and clad in a pitched surface pattern of standard corrugated and galvanized metal siding. Above this is a linear shaded clearstory window that captures the winter sun. At the southeast corner of the house, a generous mitered glass window captures sunrise views.

The home's entry is to the east under a flat, glass-covered walkway, while a masonry carport is attached to the west. One enters directly into a great room space for living and dining. A masonry fireplace in the northwest corner is the focus of this space. A wall of glass to the north looks to an open courtyard. A guest suite is to the west. In the northeast corner, a ramped gallery leads down to the master bedroom suite. The south view from this space dramatically focuses on Gavilan Peak, just beyond.

Photos: © Timothy Hursley

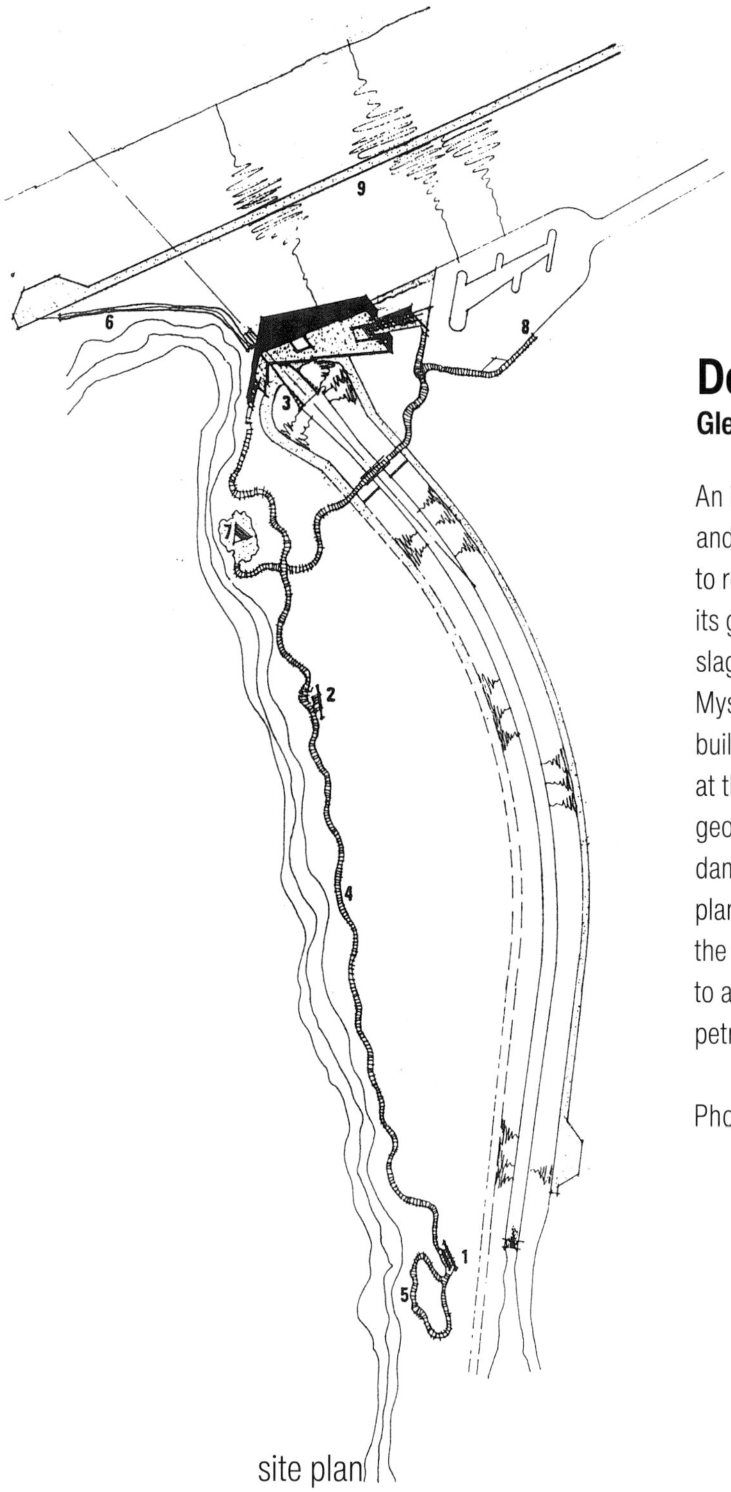

site plan

Deer Valley Petroglyph Preserve

Glendale, Arizona, 1988

An interpretive center offers exhibition, research, classroom, and curatorial space for the study of ideas and materials related to rock art. The center's architectural strength comes from its geometry and creative use of dark purple, black copper slag-encrusted concrete panels and weathered steel trellises. Mysterious and timeless, it is tuff and sensuous architecture built on subtle nuances. The building's stealth form, sited at the juncture of the Adobe Mountain Dam and the Hedgpeth Hills geologic formation, literally spans across the earthen dam's concrete outlet works. The funnel-like, boomerang-shaped plan geometry serves as a metaphorical time machine, taking the visitor from the surrounding suburban sprawl of Phoenix to a desert sanctuary, where a trail leads visitors to over 1,500 petroglyphs dating to the Hohokam culture from AD 900–1100.

Photos: © Bill Timmerman

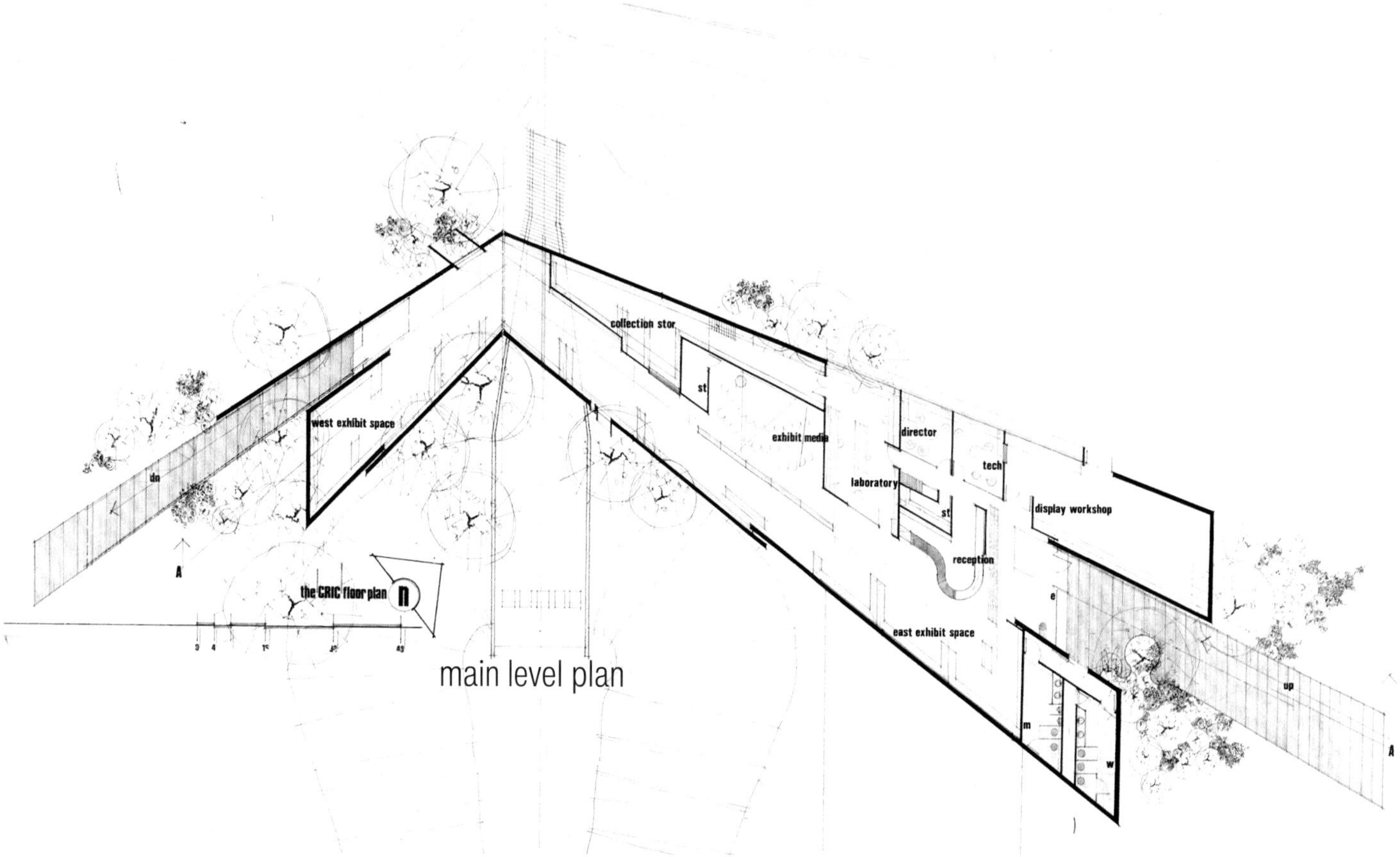

main level plan

deer valley rock art center

WHAT
why
is the past
were they made
HOW
will they last
when
can you tell
do you ask

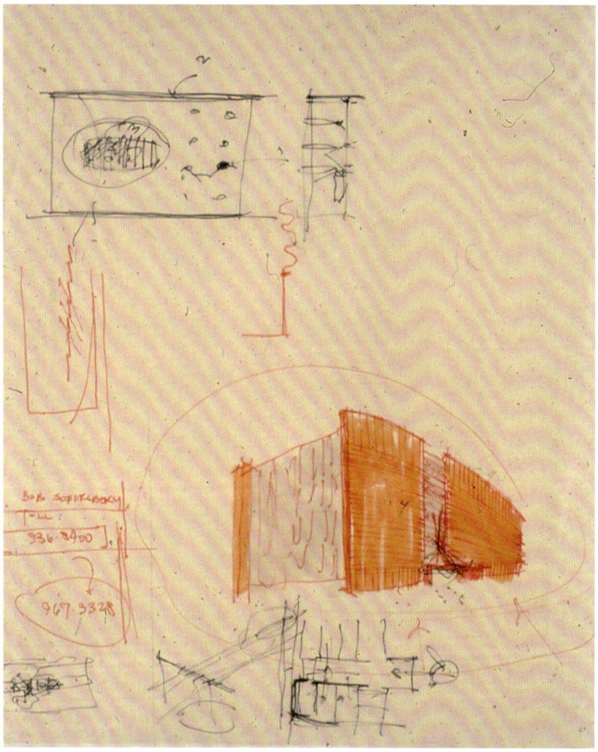

Phoenix Central Library

Phoenix, Arizona, 1989

The Phoenix Central Library has become a landmark on the Phoenix skyline and an icon of late twentieth-century modern architecture. It is celebrated as a point of community pride, serving as a nexus for the region's library and information needs.

The library houses a million-volume collection within its 280,000 square feet. Using a single small central open core, the "crystal canyon" provides vertical circulation with three high-speed elevators and the grand five-level staircase, a plan arrangement that renders all collections accessible and simple to find. The great reading room on the fifth floor, one of the largest in the US, houses the nonfiction collection. Combining innovative computer cabling, lighting, furniture design, and general collection layout strategies for presentation of the library's digital and real information, the library's unique flexibility meets normal daily changes in operation gracefully and economically.

Designed before LEED Certification existed, the library is an oft-cited example of green architecture, as it addresses many issues of environmentally sustainable design through an innovative approach to task and daylighting, thermal mass temperature control, and highly efficient mechanical systems.

At the time the library was commissioned, City of Phoenix head librarian Ralph Edwards called on the design architects to make a flexible warehouse for books, and a digital highway to knowledge; a place where ideas and services could be offered, incubate, and flourish. As on-call architects for the building, Will Bruder and his studios have repurposed and restored the library's interior spaces over the years for user groups and individuals: children (Children's Place and Garden); teens (Teen Central); makers (MACH1); college bound aspirants (College Depot); entrepreneurs (The Hive); and computer classes and user support (Computer Commons). In addition, the Pulliam Auditorium, Arizona Room Collection, and Rare Book Room continue to offer meeting spaces, while the Central Gallery showcases the work of local artists and augments the works from the Phoenix public art collection that are already installed throughout the library. Such special use spaces have become a model for public libraries across the country. The building was awarded a LEED Existing Building Silver Certificate in 2010 and garnered the prestigious AIA Twenty-five Year Award in 2021.

Photos: © Bill Timmerman, unless noted

© Will Bruder, top and middle

© Will Bruder, top and bottom

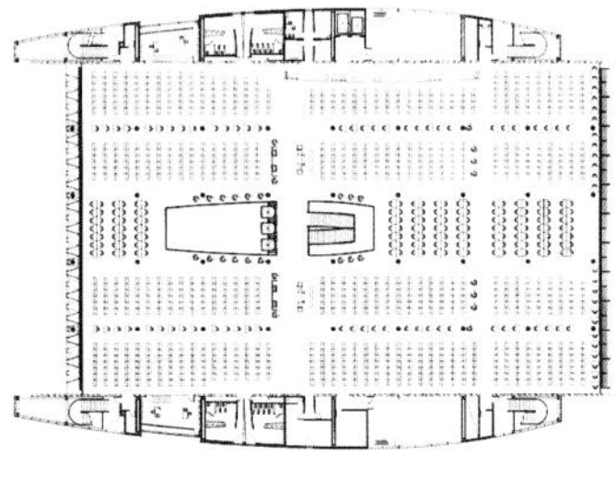

fifth floor plan

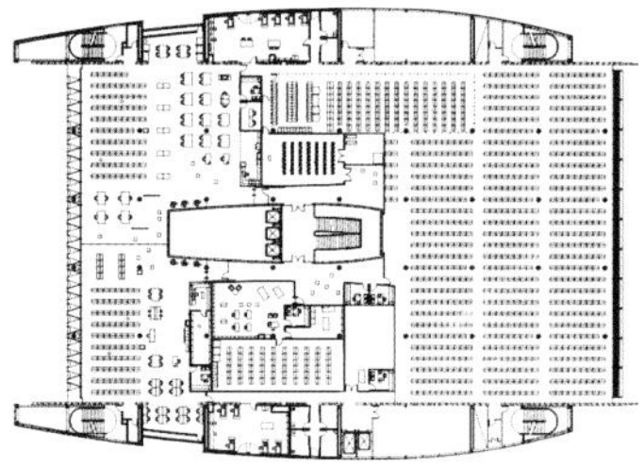

fourth floor plan

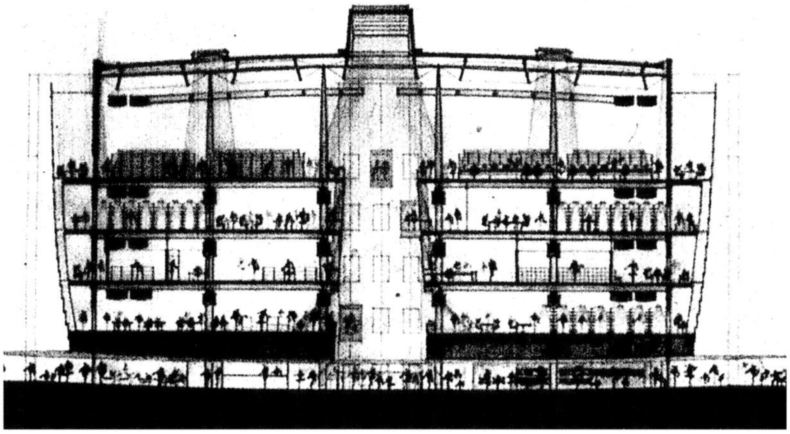

section A-A

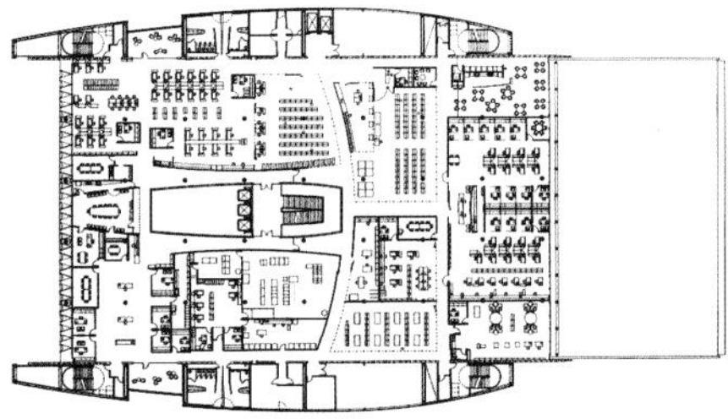

third floor plan

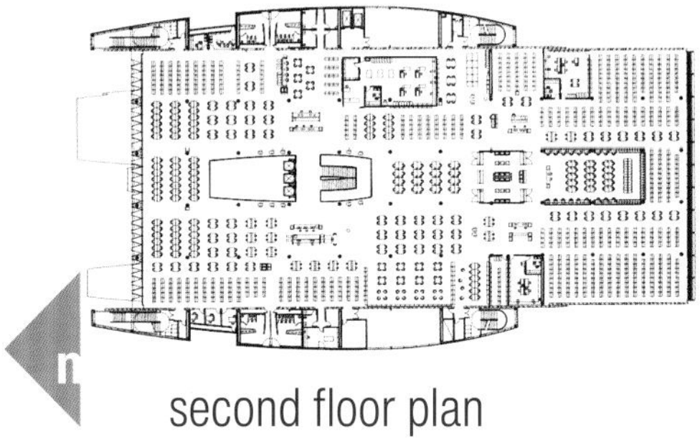

second floor plan

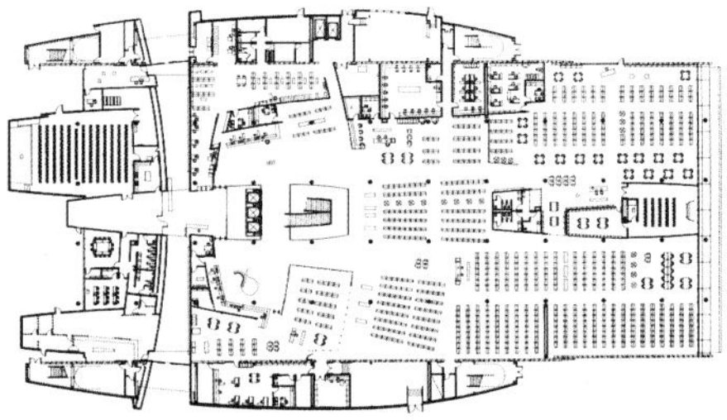

main level plan

Video

© GFreihalter/Wikimedia

© Timothy Hursley

650-745

© Will Bruder

Hill Sheppard Residence

Phoenix, Arizona, 1990

© Timothy Hursley

Perched on a steep left-over lot of challenging topography and dramatic mountain views, this suburban Phoenix residence reflects the informal character of a European hilltown. Formally, the architecture is structured around the ordering of orthogonal and trapezoidal plan moves, using reciprocating complementary angles. Sectionally, the house raises from the street as a six-leveled vessel of sorts, along an exterior/interior staircase of site-salvaged stone, crafted oak, and perforated preformed galvanized steel open treads. This stair experience draws one up to the sky, affording privileged views of Piestewa Peak from all the residence's varied spaces.

The garden courtyard voids of the house are also important, as are the strong positive galvanized metal architectural forms. These reference vernacular nineteenth-century agricultural architecture. Inside, the clients' diverse collection of Native American, folk, found object, and contemporary art flows seamlessly throughout the indoor/outdoor spaces and provides a personal and fine-grained texture to the residence's bold, colorful, and dramatic architecture.

Photos: © Bill Timmerman, unless noted

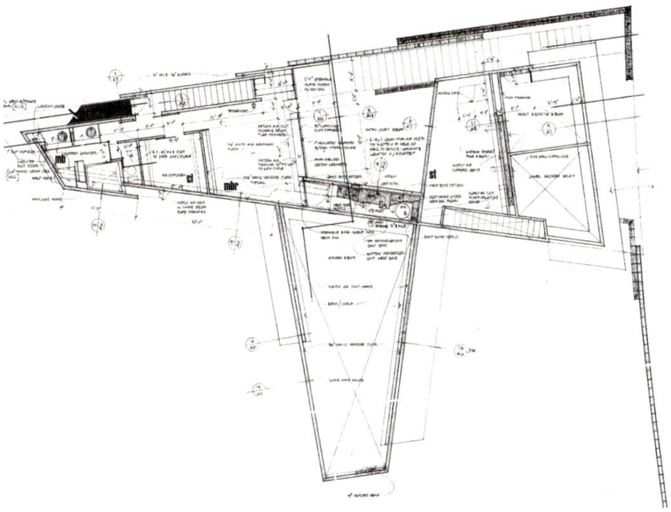

upper floor plan

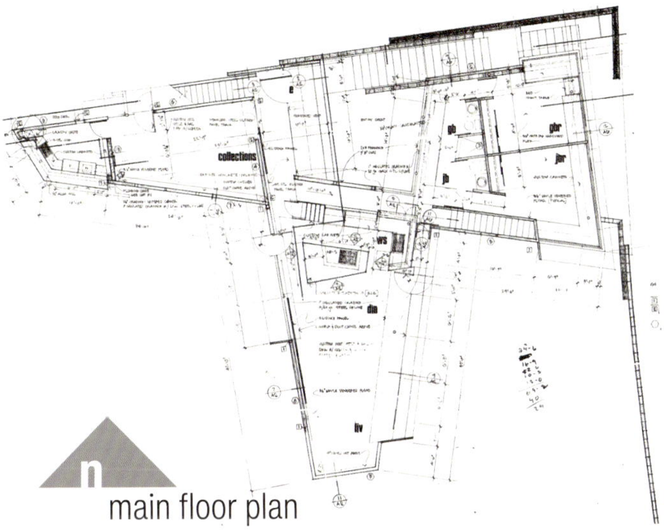

main floor plan

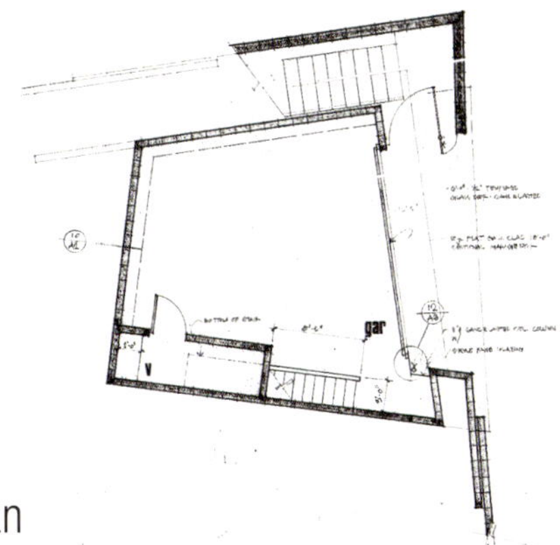

entry level plan

© Timothy Hursley

© Timothy Hursley

© Timothy Hursley

© Timothy Hursley

© amirsmier/Pixabay

© Will Bruder

Temple Kol Ami

Scottsdale, Arizona, 1992

The design intent of the Temple Kol Ami worship and learning center was to create a metaphorical village in the spirit of the ancient desert communities of Masada and Jerusalem. With the constraints of a very modest budget and the aspirations of capturing a grander symbolic presence, simple sandblasted concrete block was randomly laid to enhance its surface interest in sun and shade. This wall system is used as both the primary exterior and interior material. The compound's "street facade" (eastern wall) is, in contrast, precisely crafted as it follows and leans in a gentle and sensuous varying curve. The unique complexity of section and plan gives the sanctuary a very simple yet memorable spatial volume. A moving ray of sunlight appears through north/south-facing clerestories of the room's butterfly roof to place the worshiper in seasonal light. Classrooms along a walkway covered by a folded canopy of corrugated fiberglass are carefully scaled to the students they serve as well as animated by sunlight through clerestories.

Photos: © Bill Timmerman, unless noted

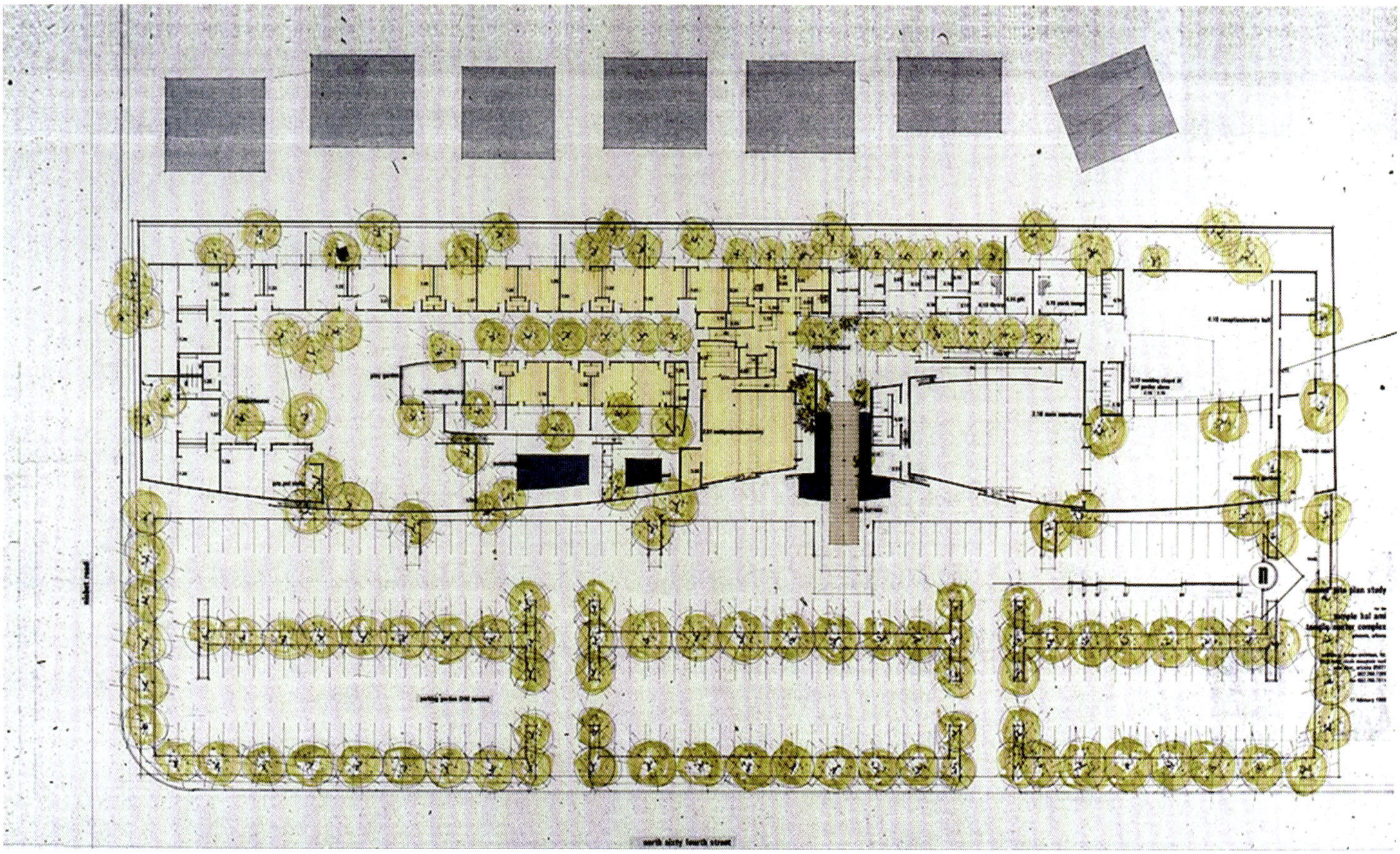

© Will Bruder

RED
ORANGE
YELLOW

© Will Bruder

Teton County Public Library

Jackson, Wyoming, 1992

The Teton County Library is a modern reinterpretation of Wyoming's vernacular ranch buildings and the log structures that still populate the region. Bruder endows an essentially simple building with humane inventiveness and lively material presence.

The library eases gently into a "wild west" landscape of rolling forested hills and snow-capped mountains. Built on the edge of the town of Jackson, Wyoming, the site is flanked to the north by a busy road. The plan is based on two wedge-shaped volumes pushed together and enveloped by a great over-sailing pitched roof, like a big log cabin or ranch house gable. Clad in rough-sawn planking, the larger wedge contains the main public volume of the library, which is conceived as a great luminous room facing south over reading decks, lawns, and a courtyard for children's storytelling. The smaller wedge, its walls rendered a deep, oxblood red, houses the library's backstage facilities, such as librarian's offices and staff rooms.

A building well suited to its rural community, it is also a new civic landmark that distills bold, tectonic poetry out of a utilitarian brief. The building's American regionalism captures a romantic pragmatism that responds energetically to both users and context.

Photos: © Bill Timmerman, unless noted

main level plan

TETON
county library

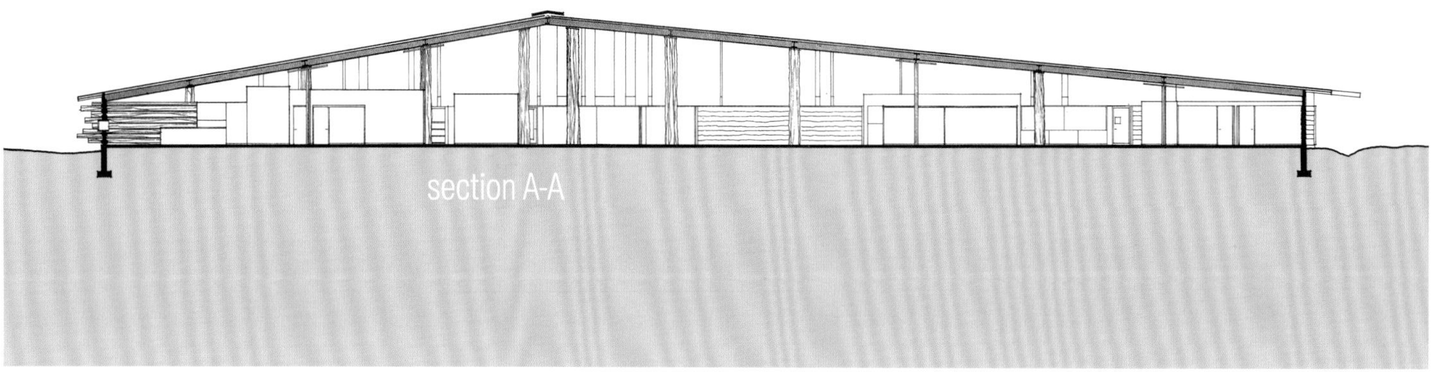
section A-A

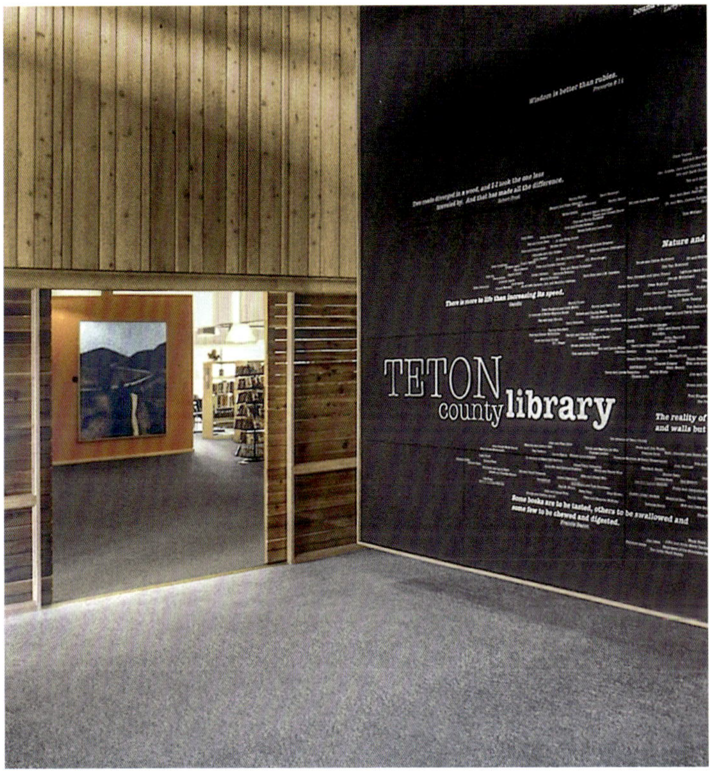
TETON
county library

children

© Will Bruder

Riddell Advertising

Jackson, Wyoming, 1993

Growing from the sprawled commercial fabric of west Jackson, the Riddell building is a celebration of the region's natural and built context. Inspired in form and material by the "muffin haystack" of surrounding ranches and the log virtuosity of Old Faithful Inn at Yellowstone National Park, the architecture is organized vertically around a skylit atrium with three massive log columns. Its curved main entrance facade responds to the sweep of the street, while the walls of its first level and two distinctive stair towers are clad in weathered random-width vertical board-and-batten cedar siding. These elements, together with a leaning preformed galvanized metal west wall, transform the ordinary vernacular "palette of the place" into a dynamically distinctive place of our time. A photography studio, project room, and lobby greet the visitor on the first level. Second-level creative and account staff workstations and third-level business offices, presentation room, library, and lunchroom all wrap the building's skylit garden "heart" while enhancing staff *esprit de corps*.

Photos: © Bill Timmerman, unless noted

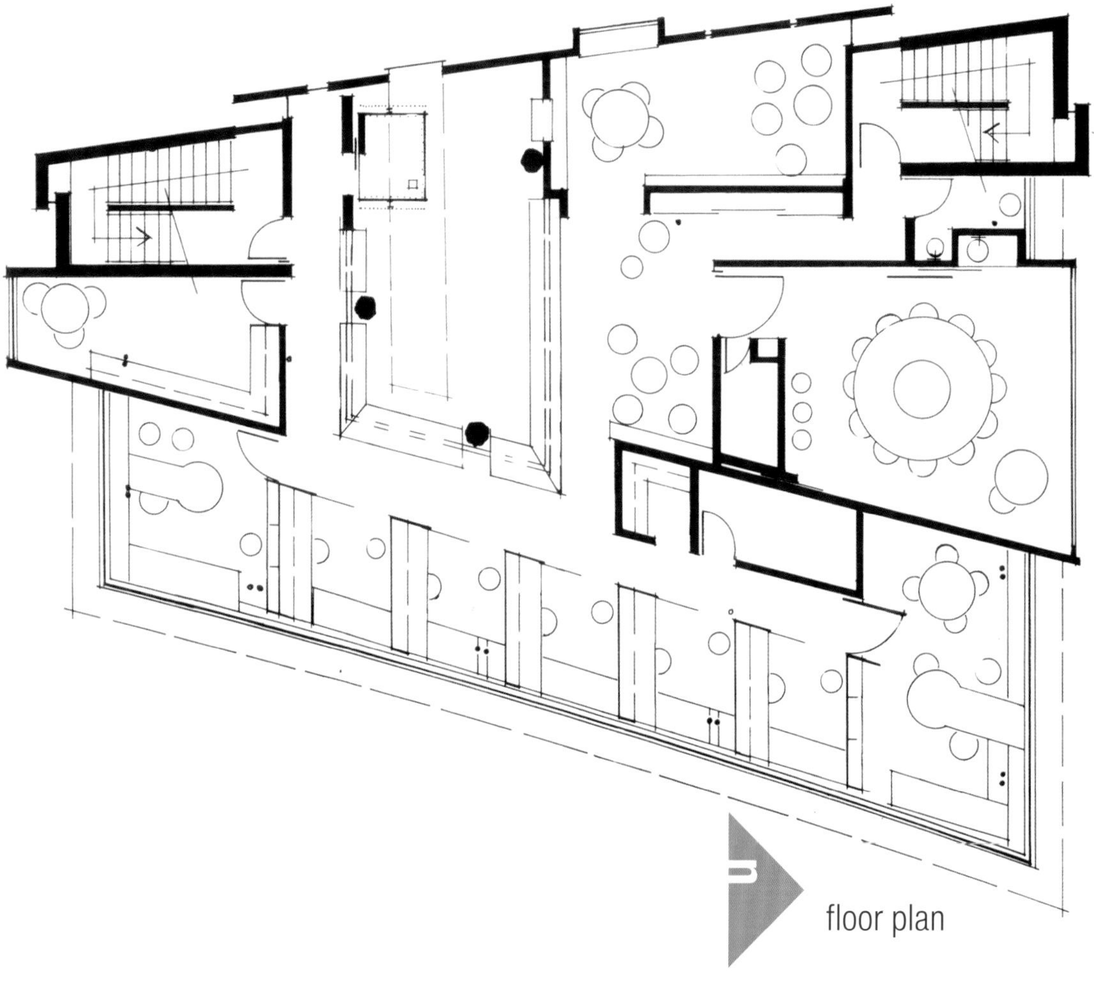

floor plan

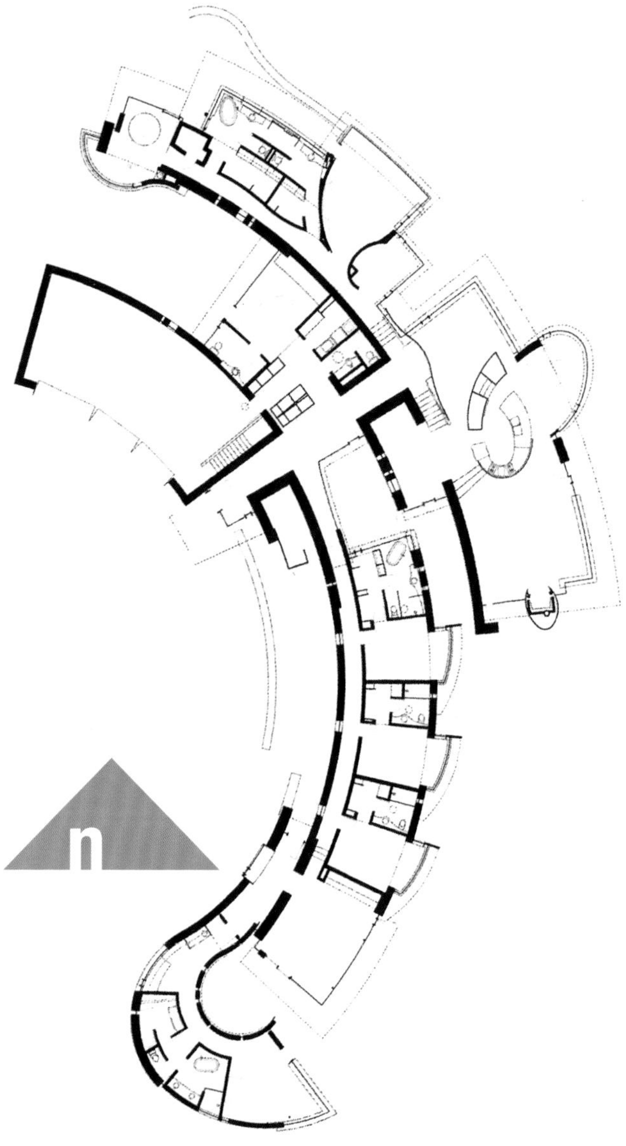

main level plan

Horne Residence, Sea Arc

Prides Crossing, Massachusetts, 1993

Overlooking the Atlantic Ocean north of Boston, Massachusetts, this residence is nestled on granite ledges at a forest's edge. The serpentine arrival path of the driveway is anchored by a loop around an aged beech tree from which the radially ordered plan of the home is zoned by multiple arcing granite walls. At the entry, the stone massing is sliced by a cantilevered stainless steel overhang that, in turn, is split by a very narrow skylight that draws you through the house to the ocean view beyond the dining room. While the main crescent contains the public living pavilion and master bedroom suite, secondary crescents hold smaller family bedrooms, and a generous guest suite.

The marriage to site continues in the sweeping vaulted-roof form of the main pavilion, evoking Northeastern boatbuilding traditions. With a radial standing-seam copper roof appearing at once earthen and nautical, its shape and dark, shell-like patina evoke memories of sea creatures and vessels. Interior pearlescent-white and royal-blue Venetian plaster carries light from a quiet, protected koi pond at the entry to the sea beyond. Warming the palette is an extensive use of mahogany and sycamore millwork and doors, richly textured furnishings, and a cast-bronze fireplace mantel by the metalsmith Darcy Miro. This living sculpture has been evolving over the course of a twenty-year collaboration between the client/patron and architect.

Photos: © Bill Timmerman

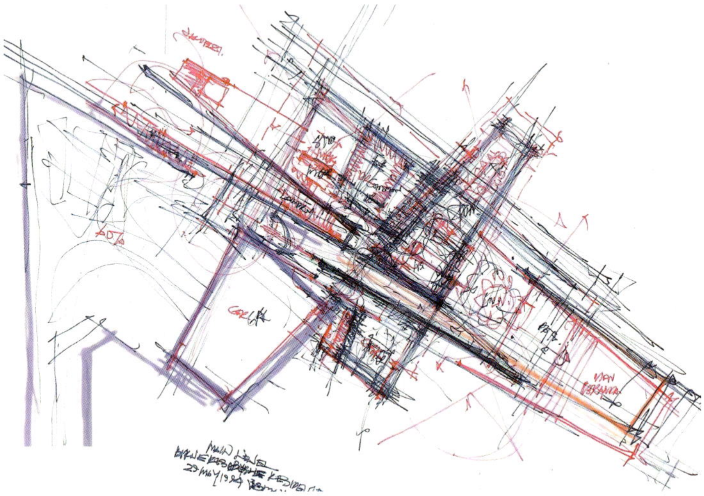

Byrne Residence
Scottsdale, Arizona, 1994

The residence is a series of abstract canyon walls and spaces that emerge as metaphoric geological gestures from its steep south-facing desert site. With dramatically corbeled concrete tilting, raking masonry, and metal-clad frame walls, the architectural embrace of the residence's main entry, living, and circulation gallery spaces is both original and invigorating. The structure's angular geometry grows from the asymmetrical, tapering alignment of a "canyon." The purple/black patinated copper, acid-etched galvanized metal-clad frame wall, and fascia elements complement the undisturbed Sonoran Desert surround. Large window walls, patios, and courtyards of shade and sun allow indoor/outdoor living throughout the desert calendar.

In its scale, sculptural form, and material simplicity, the Byrne Residence is an organic architectural statement that complements and enhances its unique desert setting.

Photos: © Bill Timmerman

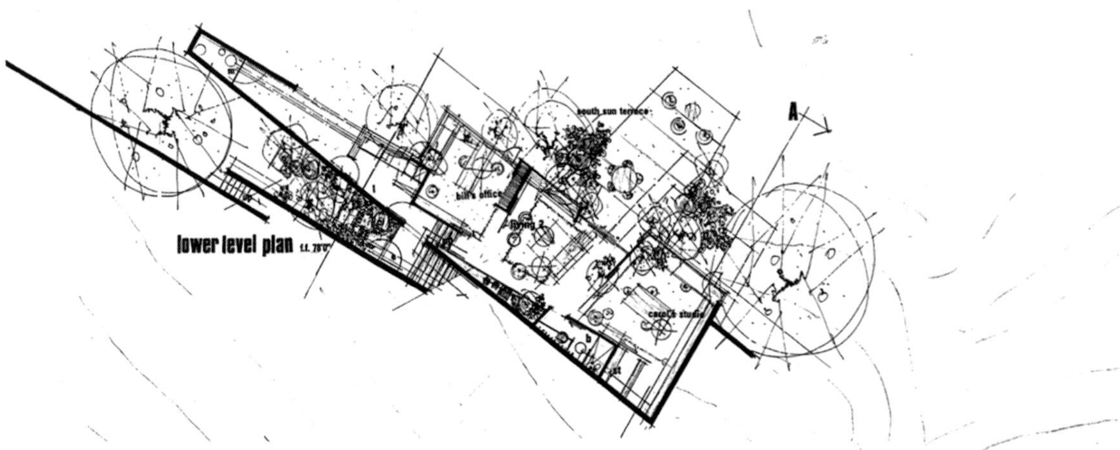
lower level plan
south sun terrace
bill's office
living 2
A

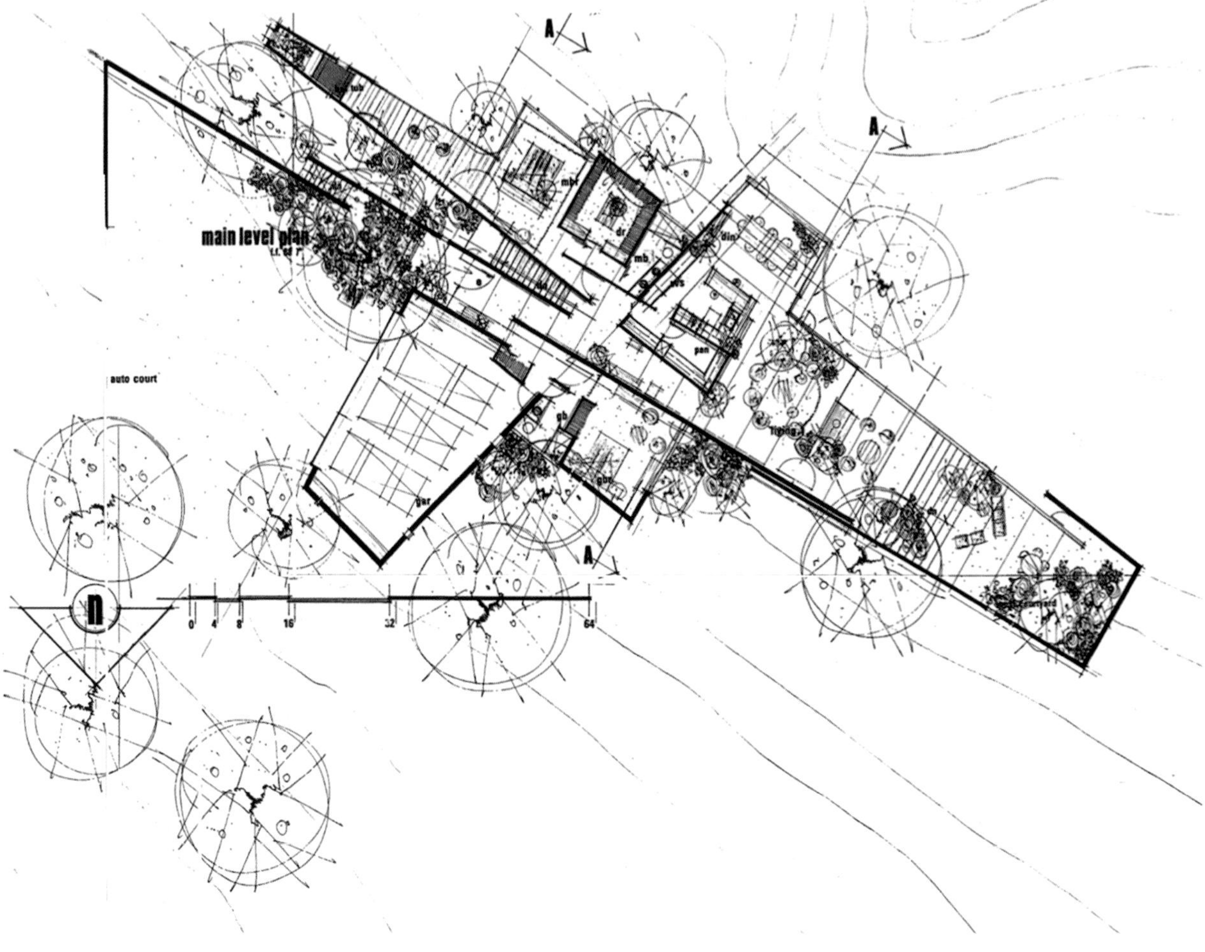
main level plan
auto court
mb
dr
din
pan
living
gar
A
n
0
4
8
16
32
64

section A-A
carol's studio

Townsend Residence

Paradise Valley, Arizona 1994

What started as the modest remodel of a 1970s pseudo-Spanish house, totally lacking in views, sited on a spectacular mountainside lot in Paradise Valley, Arizona, turned into a fully reworked "sculptural" experience. Focused on the creation of a 200-foot-long, north-facing seamless glass "horizon catcher," the architecture evolved into a fresh and highly specific armature for the clients' personal proclivities.

A processional interweaving of curved wall forms and changing volumes, bathed in natural light, loosely define the living spaces and daily flow patterns. The plan poetically captures pragmatic functional needs while evolving an inside/out/outside/in feeling of site connectivity. With its free-flowing form, the residence complements the clients' museum-quality modern furniture collection and offers a refined contrast to its jagged mountainside site.

Photos: © Bill Timmerman

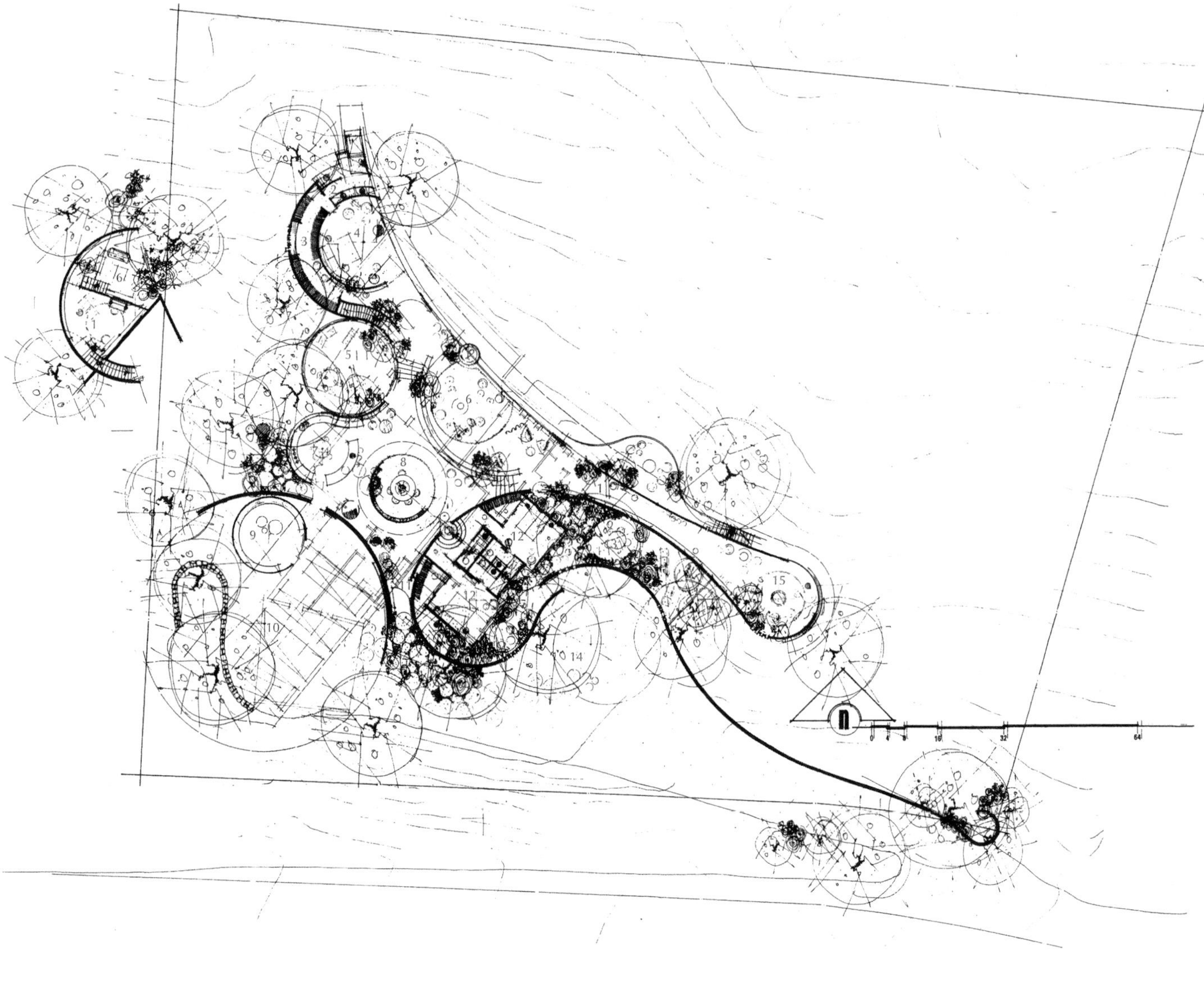
1
2
3
4
5
6
7
8
9
10
11
12
14
15
16
0
4
8
16
32
64

Mad River Rafting

Jackson, Wyoming 1995

Mad River Boat Trips is conceived as a metaphorical rusty rock, wedged alongside Flat Creek. As an extension of Snow King Mountain, its architecture draws from the straightforward structures—barns, hay sheds, and gas stations—of the Wyoming landscape, while simultaneously making a distinctive mark in an otherwise nondescript commercial highway strip. The building's minimal and transparent custom-glazed highway facade reads as a shimmering waterfall to all who pass and has become a dynamic entry marker for Jackson.

The building serves as departure lounge, headquarters, and warehouse for the staging of Mad River's white water rafting adventures on the Snake River. A rich mix of functions is housed within: a white water rafting museum, retail space, and bunkhouse for river guides (workforce housing), topped by the owner's deluxe penthouse apartment. In form, materiality, and program, the building speaks to the robustness and imagination of the owner as well as the mythic individualism of the Wyoming experience.

Photos: © Bill Timmerman

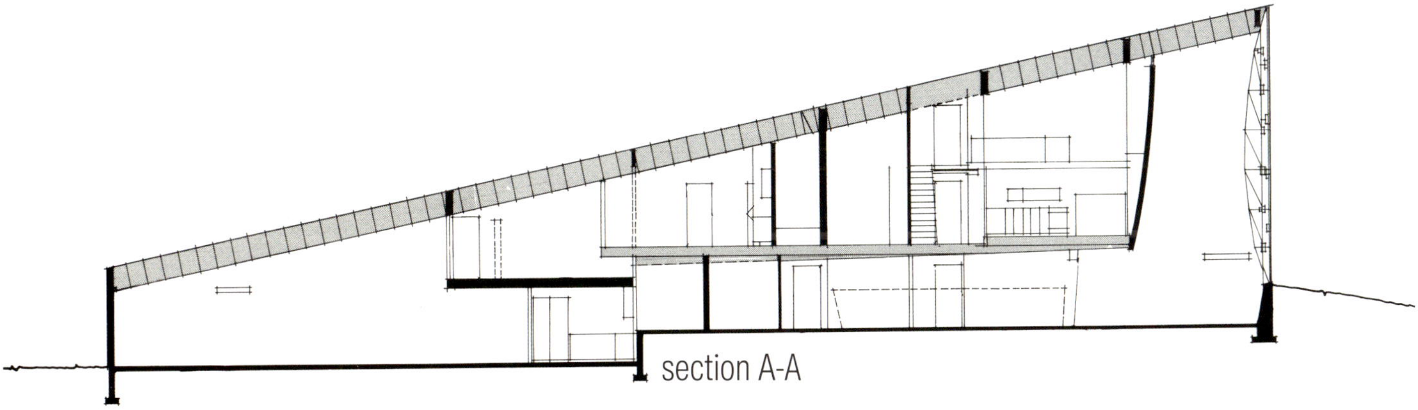
section A-A

mad river

GEORGIE
SRB I
wyoming
utah
colorado
new mexico
arizona

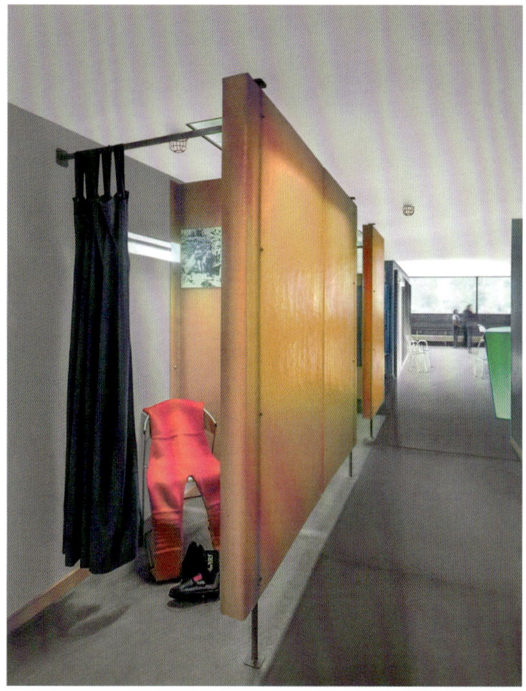

ANDE
NTS

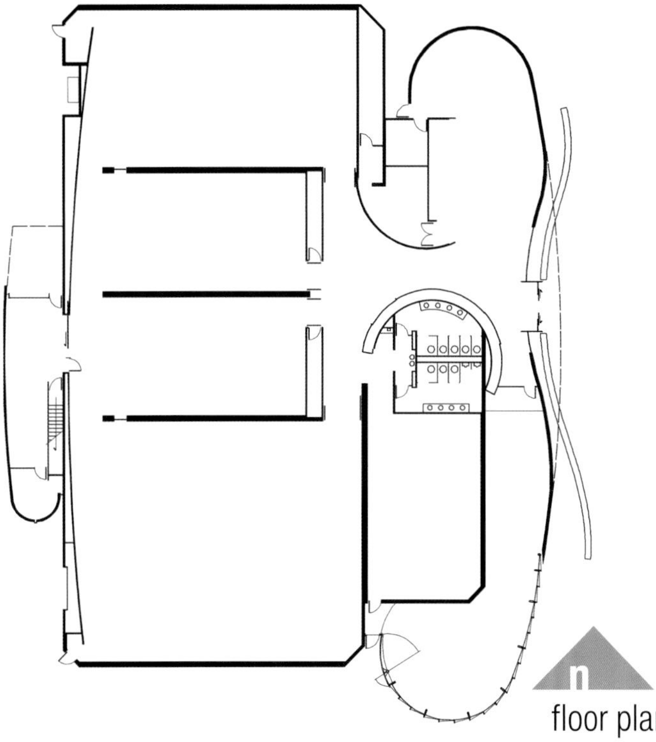

floor plan

Scottsdale Museum of Contemporary Art (SMoCA)

Scottsdale, Arizona, 1996

In this project, a former 1976 five-plex movie theater of faux Spanish style is inventively repurposed as a contemporary art museum on the cultural campus of Scottsdale, Arizona. SMoCA's entry pavilion is clad in a curving metal skin formed of randomly seamed galvanized steel panels. It pays homage to the similarly curved facades of the neighboring performing art center by Arizona master architect Bennie Gonzales. An east-facing glass entry portal opens into the museum's admission/shop area to the north and enclosed garden to the south, where sunlight plays across the scrim wall of translucent and colored dichroic glass by James Carpenter, as it embraces Knight Rise (2001), a Skyspace by James Turrell.

The interior transition zone is a refined balance of translucent, luminous light, polished concrete, blackened steel, MDF wall paneling, and overscaled custom-crafted maple gallery doors. The main galleries enjoy total flexibility for installations, varied artificial and natural lighting and state of the art climate controls, as well as a common curved western wall for easy circulation.

Photos: © Bill Timmerman, unless noted

before

before

© Will Bruder

Gerald L. Cafesjian Pavilion
scottsdale museum of contemporary art

© Will Bruder, top, middle and bottom

Jonathan & Eve Read
Goldschmidt
Michael & Suzanne Fromkin
the Sheldon R. Roth Family
Stephen & Gail Rineberg
Naomi Caras-Miller & Alvin Miller
Sara & David Lieberman
Northern Trust Bank
Michael Ash
The Scottsdale Tribune
Michael & Ellie Ziegler
Bank One, Arizona
Robert & Sue Karatz
PCS Health Systems, Inc.
Salt River Project
America West Airlines
Carlisle SynTec, Inc.
Wells Fargo Bank

admission & membership
museum store

MESA CITY
MACRO-COSANTI

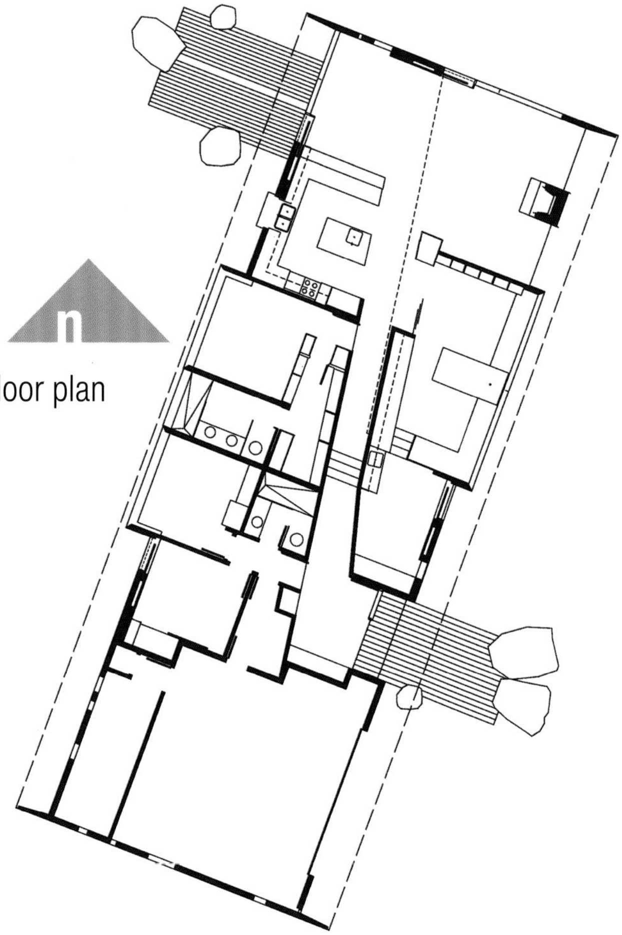

floor plan

Riddell Residence/Rural

Wilson, Wyoming, 1999

Celebrating the clients' shared passion for the outdoors and the needs of a painter, a photographer, and their special dog, this modest wooden residence is a refined and poetically organized shelter for life, work, and leisure. This long, low structure has an immediately apparent asymmetrical ridge gable that reinterprets the vernacular forms of neighboring ranch service buildings. Narrow, vertical reveal-jointed resawn weathered cedar boards catch the light and patina of time, with the black stains from the carefully placed iron nails giving the wooden siding the linear rigor of an Agnes Martin painting. Small square window apertures framed in thin, polished stainless steel catch the color and reflections of changing light, while the large floor-to-ceiling glass walls offer views into the surrounding conifer and aspen woods. Simple white walls, slate and wood floors, and refined cabinetry of maple create a backdrop for sensuous furnishings, art, and personal collections.

Photos: © Bill Timmerman

Nevada Museum of Art (NMA)

Reno, Nevada 1999

© Grant Mudford

The Nevada Museum of Art creates a dynamic urban presence in downtown Reno. The Museum frames a series of well-scaled and formed galleries and references the geologic formations of the nearby Black Rock Desert. The carefully lapped, handcrafted random seam pattern of Anthra-Zinc applied over the west facades exaggerates the form of the building with a unique organic tapestry of shade and shadow. Entry into the Museum is through a compressed wedge of intimately scaled walls inserted under the raked black ceiling of the first-level public spaces. The visitor is at once inside and outside in a glass pavilion and four-story skylight atrium, carving through the entire section of the building. Lifting one's eyes upward, the atrium is an ever-changing chamber of form, light, and shadow. The roof terrace sculpture garden caps the atrium and staircase, and is formed by the edges of the building as they sweep up on a rake to the sky where the syncopated rhythm of parapet crenellations to the west frame the city, the sky, and the distance views of the Black Rock Desert.

Photos: © Bill Timmerman, unless noted

© Will Bruder

© Grant Mudford

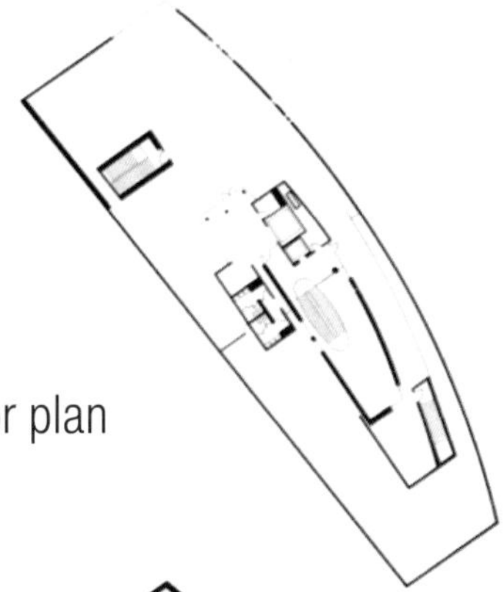

top floor plan

upper floor plan

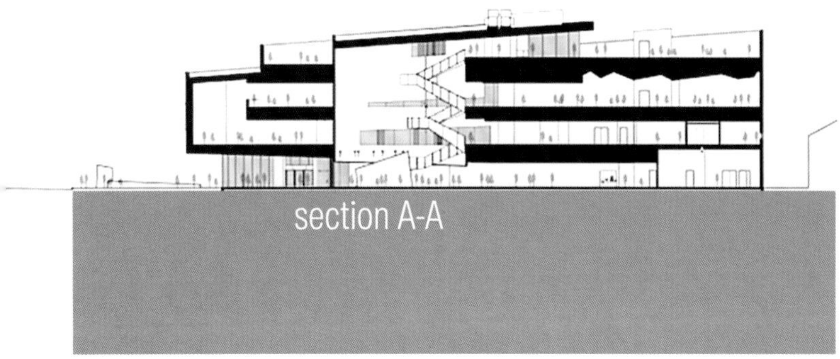

section A-A

first floor plan

entry level plan

N
NEV MUS OF
ADA EUM ART

© Grant Mudford

© Grant Mudford

© Will Bruder, top and bottom

© Will Bruder

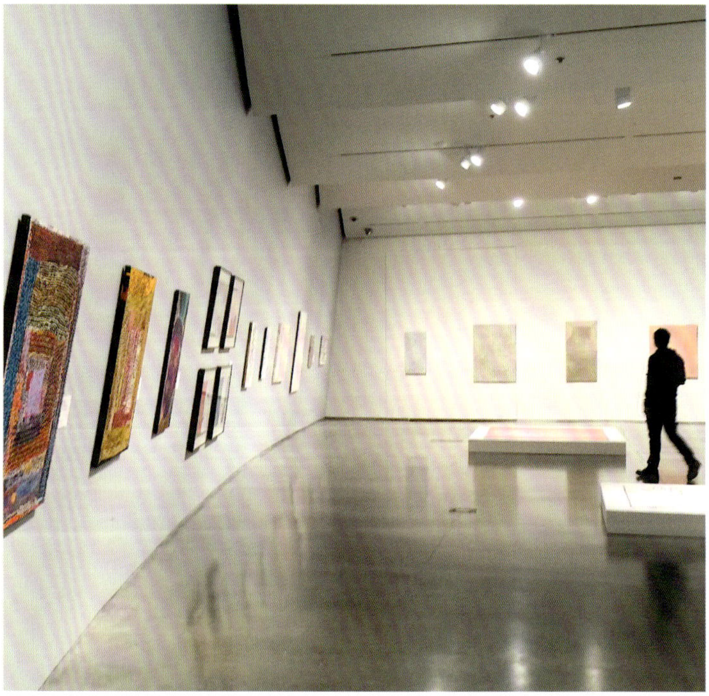

© Grant Mudford

ON SKY PLAZA
FOUNDATION

E.L. CORD MUSEUM

Nevada Museum of Art Expansion

Reno, Nevada 2025

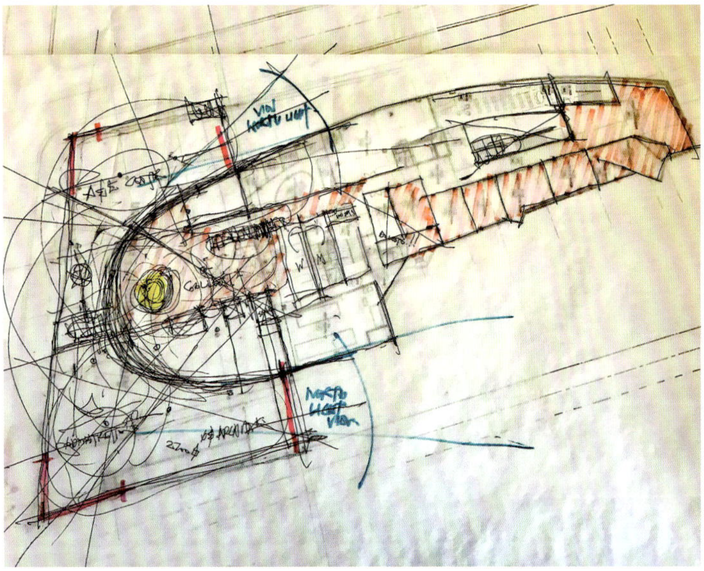

In 2025, the Nevada Museum of Art completed a 50,000-square-foot addition and reprogramming of the institution's flagship building. A dark palette, glazed apertures, and weathered steel extend the architectural vocabulary of the original building —completed in 2003. The addition's primary cladding material is black ironspot ceramic tile. The family of tiles, selected for their varying texture and size, are laid up randomly with both front and back sides of the tile facing out. This sets up a complex quilt of texture that catches and refracts available light as it changes, often dramatically, from hour to hour, day to day, season to season, in the high desert city of Reno, Nevada.

With the addition complete, the Nevada Museum of Art now occupies the city block. The new south entry is announced by a generous canopy that invites the public in and increases accessibility for daily school group visitors. A connective path through the first floor links the new south entry, gallery, and public spaces to those in the pre-existing north entry area. The three-level expansion doubles opportunities for viewing and interacting with the museum's collections on levels two and three to allow an enhanced experience of the museum's collection and curation. Elevated outdoor spaces accommodate sculpture and nurture in an indigenous garden. A new interactive library, expanded Art and Environment Archive/Research Center, open storage educational facilities, and bookstore were also part of the expansion. The result is not only an expansion of space but an expanded vision of what a museum can be in the burgeoning city of Reno.

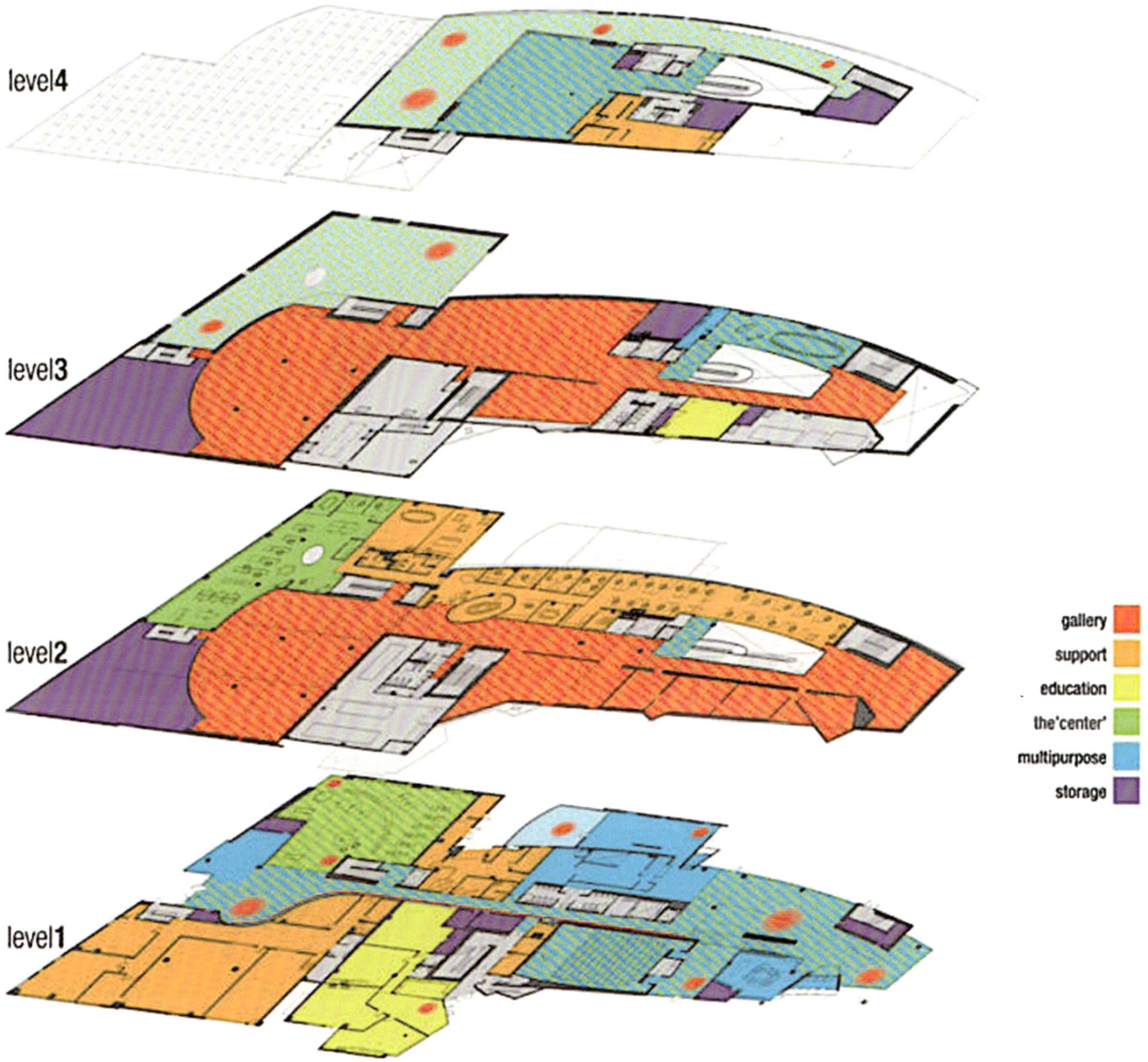
level4
level3
level2
level1
gallery
support
education
the'center'
multipurpose
storage

Renderings by Bob Neely/LJC

© Will Bruder

main level plan

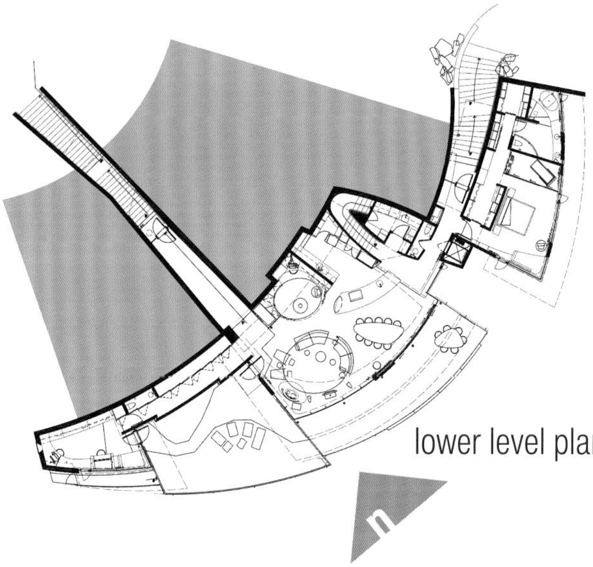

lower level plan

Kursh Piccioni Residence, Sky Arc

Marin County, California, 1999

This crescent plan house is embedded in the side of a steep slope along a curving driveway easement to a neighboring site, giving an urbane scale to the architecture while referencing the surrounding soft hillside vistas. Its simple volumes, clad in pre-weathered pewter-gray zinc with accents of wood and generous glazing, blend into the texture and colors of the landscape. The upper-level entry chamber enjoys a framed east bay view that ties the interior to its natural surroundings and the horizon. From there, a sequence of public and private spaces unfolds, filled with natural light and shadow and sensual freshness. Descending into the open-plan living area below, the house expands seamlessly on to a cantilevered wood deck and man-made lawn terrace. Boundaries dissolve into the landscape through perforated metal railings and distinctive shade brows of watery, aqua translucent, fiberglass resin that color the light of the day. A private music studio on the western edge of the site is accessed through a tunneled umbilical (under the driveway), with a landscaped play garden that looks to the surrounding views over the low rooftop profile and to Mount Tamalpais to the west.

Photos: © Bill Timmerman

Pond House

Cave Creek, Arizona, 2002

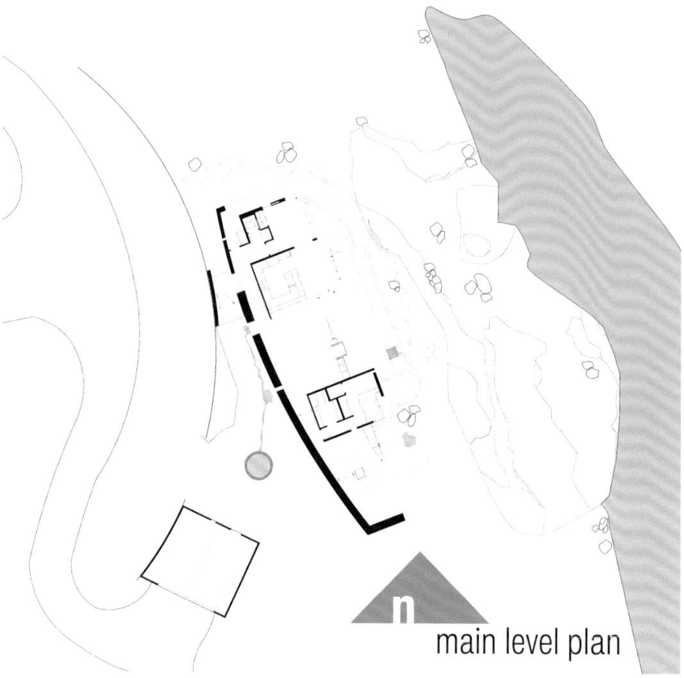

This weekend retreat grows from the upper Bajada desert landscape sited on a perennial watering hole in Cave Creek, Arizona. Metaphorically, the design reflects both ancient ruins of primitive stone construction and the weathered steel shards of nineteenth-century mining camp glory. An asymmetrical gabled roof spans between a long, curving raked stonewall and a folded wall of shaded glazing to anchor the residence to its site. Stepping down into the residence from the desert along a fountain seep, the indoor and outdoor living area of the home cantilevers out above the cool, tree-filled riparian oasis. Its intimately scaled spaces focus to distant mountain views, as exposed concrete floors, stonewalls, plywood ceilings, and a sculptural red Venetian plaster form centers the interior. An environment of careful details, comfortable scale, and elegant simplicity, the Pond House forms a contemplative retreat for its owner and all who visit.

Photos: © Bill Timmerman

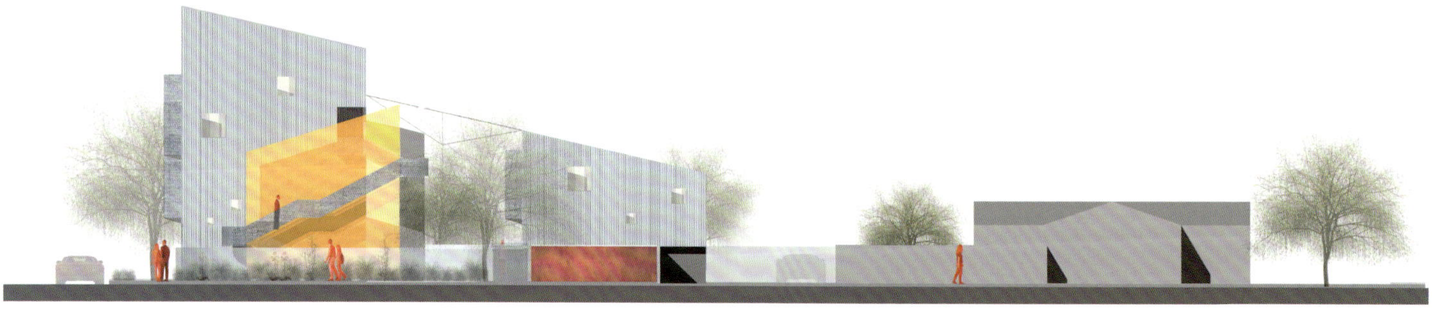

west elevation

The Vale

Tempe, Arizona, 2002

The Vale is a mixed-use commercial/residential project that broke new ground on density, street presence, and neighborhood respect, requiring thirteen variances to accomplish. Its north-facing four-story facade sits directly parallel to a busy arterial street offering mixed-use retail and live/work business with access to street parking near Tempe's downtown and the Arizona State University campus. Carriage houses above garages align the alley, providing a scale transition to the profile of older, single-family houses to the south. Underground parking provides an opportunity to maximize the site's functional potential. Over a dozen different floor plans are represented in the forty-six residential units. Private patios and terrace spaces are complemented by a shared native plant garden forming a courtyard walk of color, shade, and light that runs the length of the project to the community room and swimming pool. Street presence and identity are garnered through the use of bold "pungently optimistic" green wall planes that add energy and a playful personality to the public realm.

Photos: © Bill Timmerman

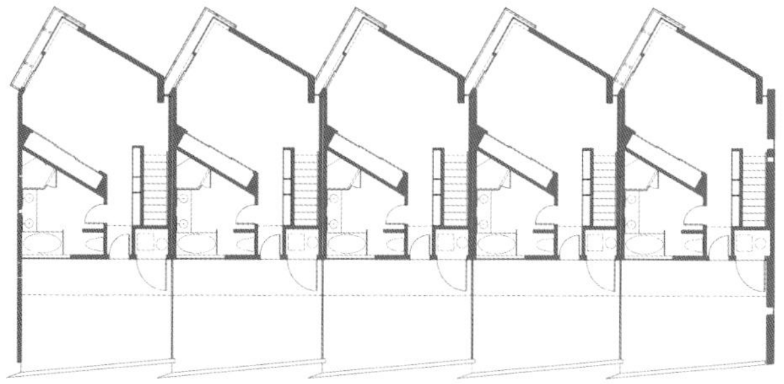

upper level plan

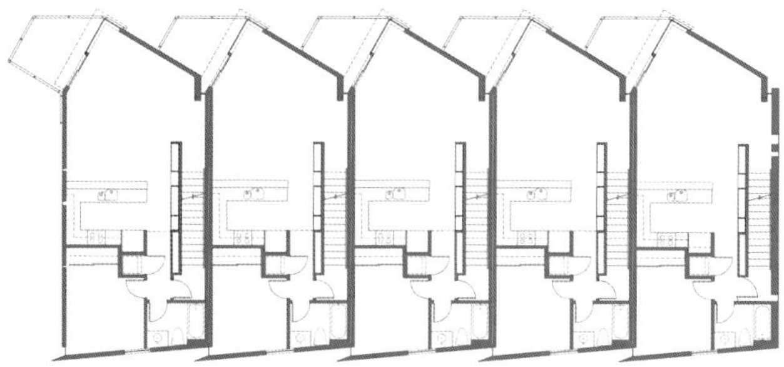

middle level plan

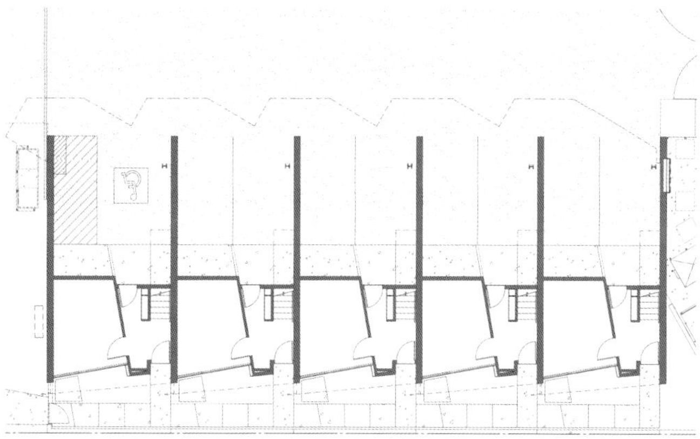

ground floor plan

Loloma 5

Scottsdale, Arizona, 2002

On a small empty lot in the single-story fabric of downtown Scottsdale, this live/work multiple of five units optimizes the site's potential through efficient use of repetitive modules and three-level sectional invention. Capturing the privileged view of the area's iconic Camelback Mountain to the northwest for all five units through the development of a folded glass facade protected by dense, but porous, scrims of perforated galvanized sheeting, Loloma 5 is rich as an urban form. With a street facade of Rheinzink standing-seam panels and variable with glazing slots on a concrete masonry first-level foundation. The dynamism of its folded north face and the rich rust patina of its secondary corrugated-metal skins complement and stand out in the context of the neighboring elegant Spanish colonial-style Loloma School of 1927, and Vito Acconci's transit center public art intervention of 1997.

Photos: © Bill Timmerman

3707

Hercules Public Library

Hercules, California, 2003

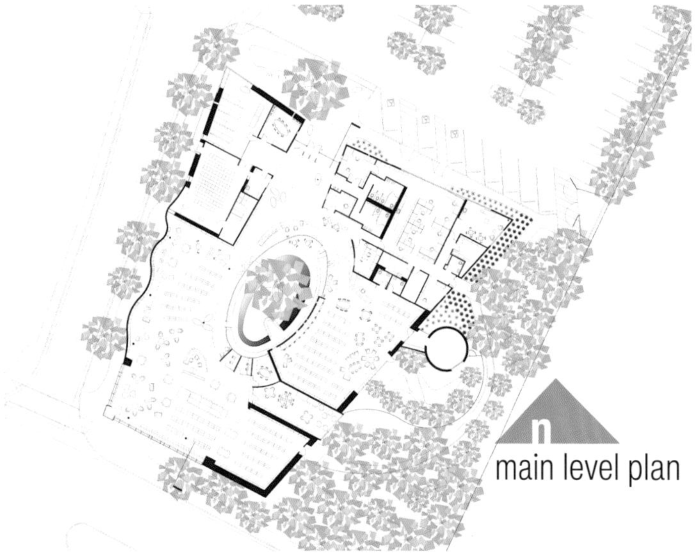

main level plan

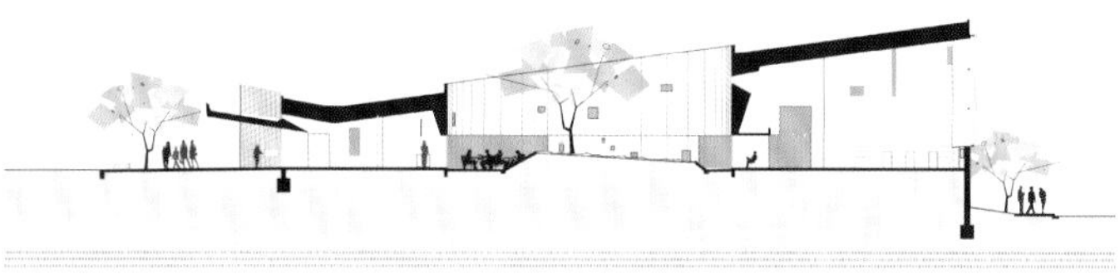

section A-A

The Hercules Public Library was conceived to be a landmark public building, a welcoming community-gathering place, and a functional, efficient vessel of knowledge and exploration in a fast-growing and highly diverse community on the north end of San Francisco Bay. Sited on a raised plinth of land overlooking a strip big box retail center on the edge of residential suburban sprawl, the library is a highly visible glazed beacon of glass and color, visible from the freeway. The building's variegated tapestry-like skin of vertical brick plate cladding is punctuated by a large, fritted glass corner window that illuminates the reading room. This window offers long views and positions the library as a place of public pride in the grassy rolling hills that surround it. Architecturally inspired by the massive adobe-walled, tile-roofed Spanish missions of sixteenth-century California, and the contemplative garden courtyard tradition of Asian homes, the library celebrates the diverse ethnic roots of the community. A large elliptically shaped garden courtyard, with its mounded moss and singular magnolia tree, is visible and accessible from the heart of the building. This quiet seating area offers a wind-sheltered oasis carefully calibrated to catch the winter sun. Computer labs, community meeting rooms, study hall spaces, and a tall, midnight-blue "story cone" provide an environment of welcome and discovery for users of all ages.

Photos: © Bill Timmerman

Hercules Public Library

fiction
information / borrower

Pool Residence

Reno, Nevada, 2003

Growing from a barren ridge, this minimalist sculpture is composed of two shed-roofed masonry boxes dynamically connected by a galvanized metal entry gallery and trellis of angular geometries.

The eastern mass of the house contains garages, guest quarters, gym, and home office. The north-facing pavilion/dining/kitchen wraps around an elliptical media cave. The west end of this pavilion contains a vertical library, master bedroom suite, and an additional cantilevered bedroom suite. Tying the two masonry pavilions together is a ramped linear entry displaying the owner's collection of art photography.

The expressive exterior presence is softened by an interior of reflective grey concrete floors and luminous white walls. Carefully located and proportioned apertures frame views of intimate desert detail, distant vistas, and the crystalline light of the high desert air. Interior furnishing selections, minimal cable light system, and inventive installation of the photo collections bring a sensual and fine-grained nuance to the bold moves of the architecture.

Photos: © Will Bruder, unless noted

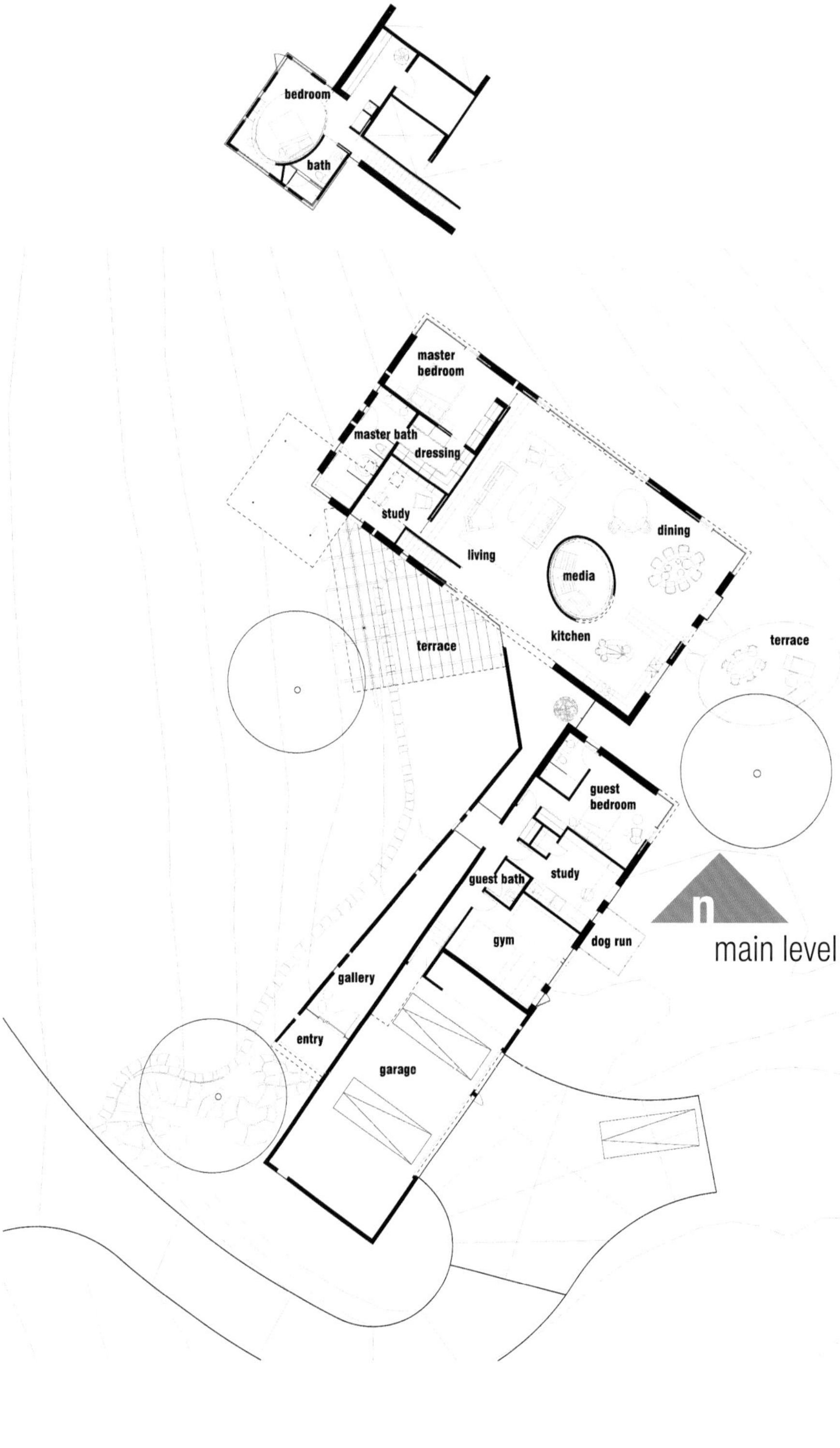

main level plan

© Yoshio Futagawa/GA, top and bottom

© Yoshio Futagawa/GA

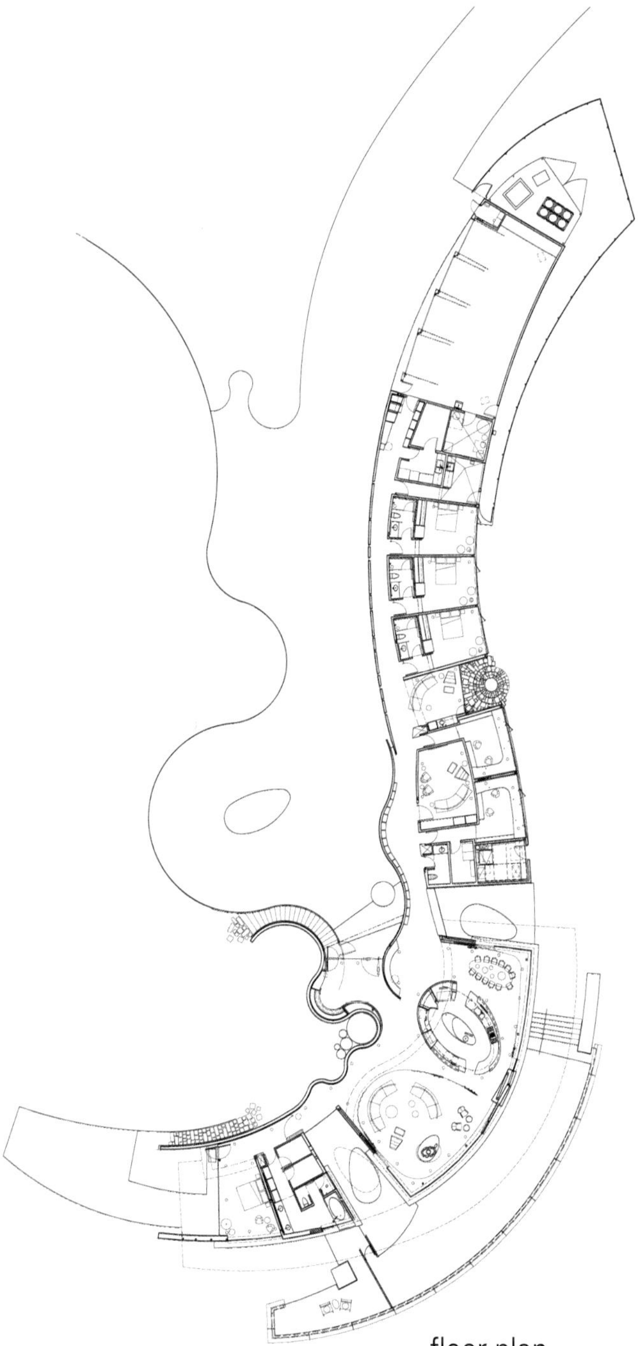

floor plan

n

Feigin Residence

Reno, Nevada, 2003

Flowing along the undisturbed topographic contours of the arid, rocky landscape above Reno, Nevada, this residence is an essay in form and movement stretched and measured along a serpentine line. The client grew up in Southern California where he was exposed to and intrigued by the work of John Lautner (1911–94), a student of Frank Lloyd Wright. Upon realizing the financial resources to commission his own home on a unique Reno building site. Impressed with the drawings and models for the proposed Nevada Museum of Art, the client commissioned a home of his own.

Approached in the daylight from the street below along an S-shaped drive, the house appears once, disappears, and reappears again, while at night it suggests a linear lantern, glowing in the landscape.

Upon arrival, a man-made canyon cleaves the landscape between the curving weathered steel retaining wall and anodized aluminum plate cladding. Entering through a graceful constriction between these faux canyon walls, the main living space's 220-degree glazed window provides views to the eastern mountain horizon. Polished concrete floors and waxed white Venetian plaster walls and ceilings complement scrims of clear frit and translucent glass. Diaphanous curtains and colored resin doors offer sensual delight. A downslope floating lawn tray projects from the living pavilion towards the horizon. The egg-shaped open kitchen is placed askew to the plan's radial geometry between the living and dining spaces. A single-loaded curving corridor to the north links the open living spaces to more private areas for sleep, media, home office, plus guest and pet accommodations. Views of the landscape are offered throughout, while gardens of moss and bamboo, an open-sky water court, a floating fire circle, and intimate sitting areas offer privacy and visual delight between program functions. Accessed from a hidden staircase, a rooftop garden provides a 360-degree view of the dramatic surrounding landscape.

Photos: © Undine Pröhl, unless noted

© Yoshio Futagawa/GA

© Yoshio Futagawa/GA

site plan

Agave Branch Library
Phoenix, Arizona, 2004

This branch library, sandwiched between a strip retail center and a beige stucco subdivision, draws in palette and construction from the language of its neighbors. Stacked bond concrete masonry units and glass enclose the simple rectangular volume of hand-troweled concrete floors, sandblasted CMU walls, exposed gang-nail trusses, Glulam beams, steel pipe columns, and painted gypsum board partitions.

In the tradition of fledgling Western frontier banks, post offices, and city halls, whose dignified, yet paper-thin, street facades belie their utilitarian construction, the library's "false front" respects both the limited budget and the large civic pride. In the open plan, a sculpture by Kendall Buster hovers above the single circulation desk, while illuminated banners assist in wayfinding. A twisting white plaster "story tower" invites pre-reader fantasy and a south-facing desert garden offers a relaxed reading spot.

Agave Branch Library addresses issues of excellence and affordability in sustainable design while raising the palette of the ordinary to that of the inspiring, comfortable, and memorable.

Photos: © Bill Timmerman

library
23550

main level plan

self check-out
dvds

magazines

copy
copia copia copi
copy
copy
copy

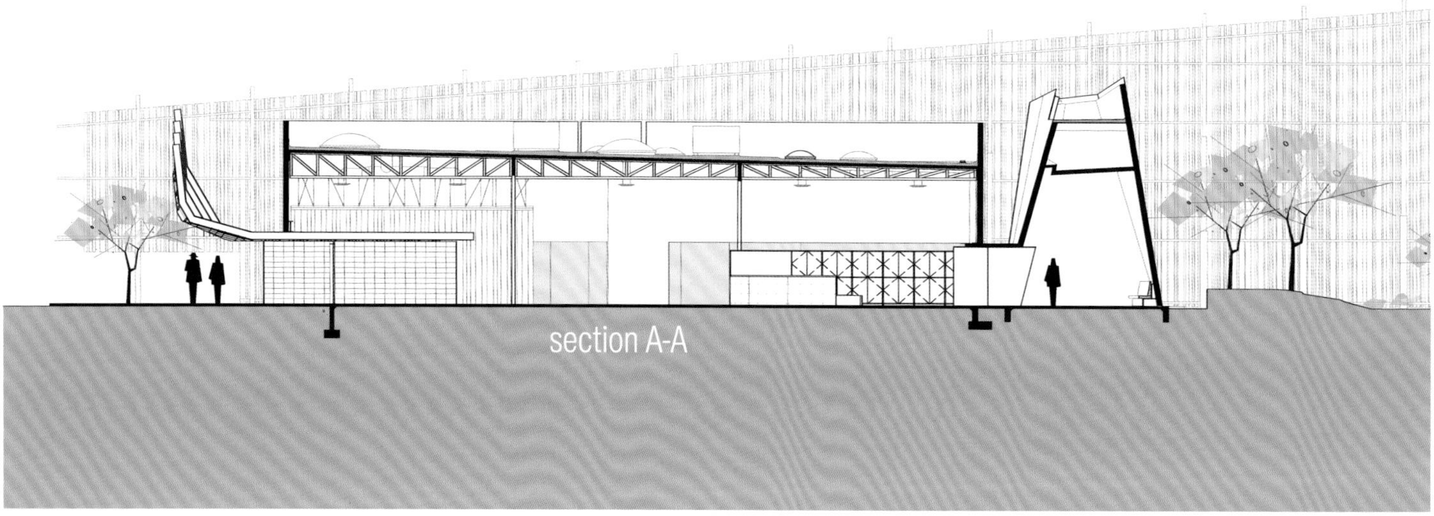
section A-A

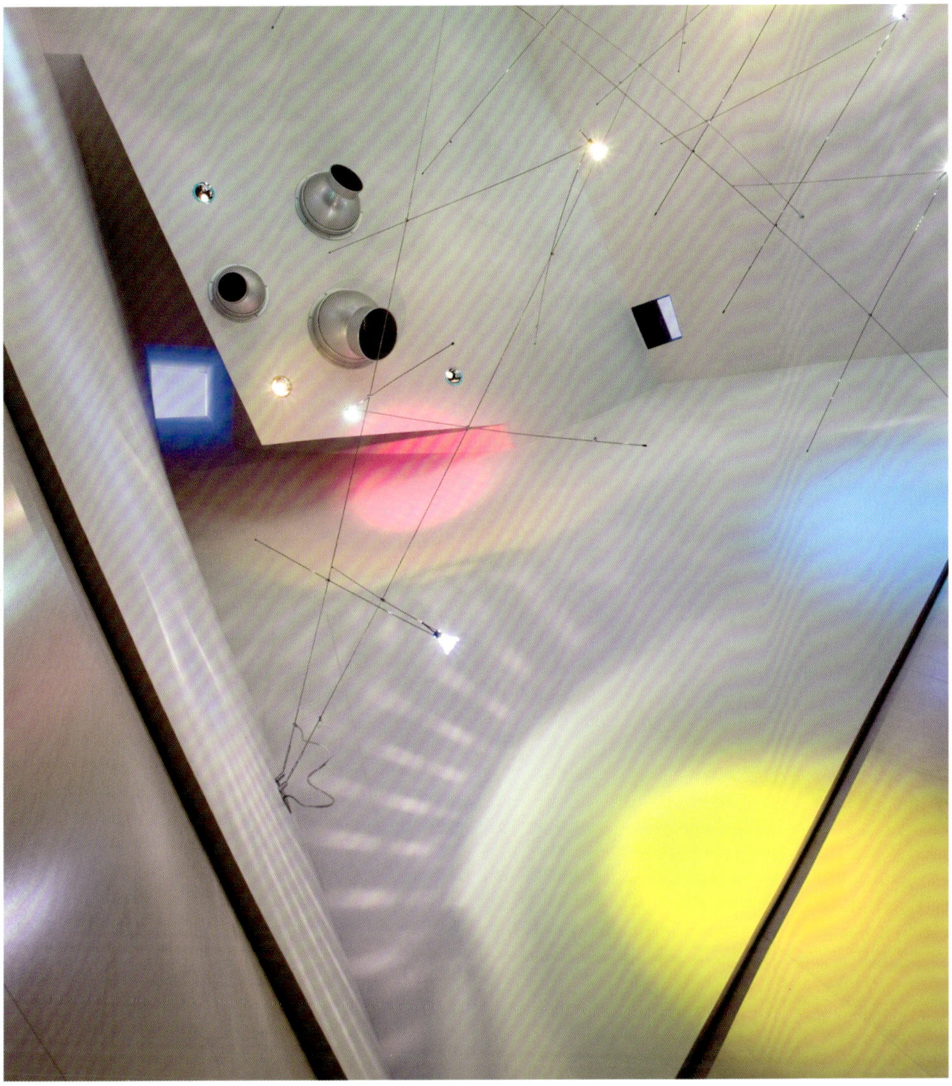

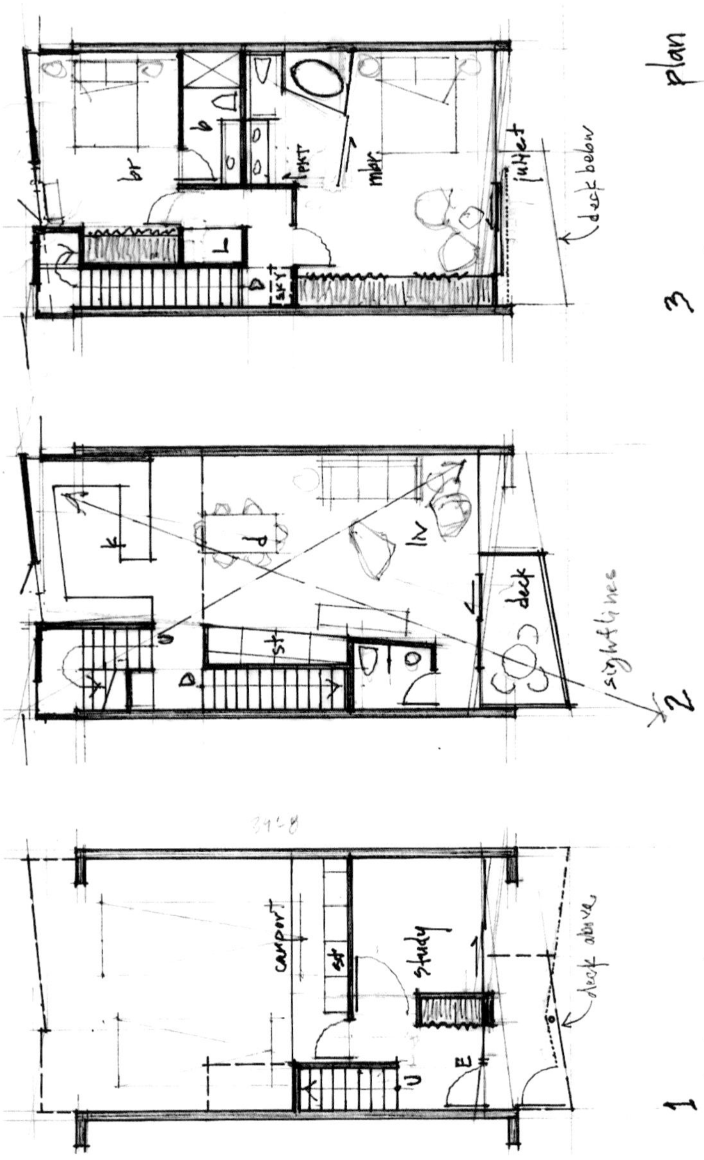

Mezzo

Phoenix, Arizona, 2005

MEZZO is the result of an enlightened and impassioned developer client supporting a design approach that grows from the outside in, and the inside out. With a total of ten units, the condo complex fits distinctively into its 1950s mid-town Phoenix residential neighborhood. Five units are entered from the east through street-side garden courtyards defined by weathered welded wire mesh. The other five units are accessed from the west along a common mews walkway of broken concrete slab pavers. At the heart of the complex is a shared auto court and raised bed community vegetable garden.

Each home of 1,525 square feet provides for entry/homework/play/carport at level 1, living/dining/kitchen at level 2, and two bedroom and bath suites at level 3. Constructed of expressed masonry bearing walls and wood frame, the units' simply sculpted spaces are given memorable identity through the use of carefully positioned window apertures, shaded by perforated metal scrims, and triangular pop-out kitchen bay windows. Angular geometries of interior walls add to the dynamism and interest of the interiors. Interior finishes of sandblasted block and painted gypsum board, stone floor, and cherry cabinets are complemented by carefully considered and crafted details.

Exterior finishes and textures of masonry and metal play against the project's dramatically positioned planes of colored plaster. In its scale and proportion, massing and materiality, and with its finely articulated details, MEZZO carves out its own unique place in this eclectic neighborhood while offering comfortable and urban living appropriate to the desert climate.

Photos: © Bill Timmerman

Jarson Residence

Paradise Valley, Arizona, 2005

This house is designed as a vessel of personal discovery for two real estate professionals with an educated passion for modern architecture, and their two sons. Gracefully embracing the topographic fold of a mountainside in the Phoenix mountains, the house focuses on the northeasterly view of the McDowell Mountains in the distance over the skyline of Scottsdale, Arizona.

With its simple shed roof and deep overhangs, the house is a sculptural form of weathered steel and copper.

Entry, office, and bedrooms are on the upper level, with the primary living and dining experience, a media/music chamber, and a potter's studio tucked beneath. Cork and concrete floors, wall planes of translucent glass, and cabinets of cherry and stainless steel articulate the interiors. The upper-level entry and passage are conceived as galleries for the owners' art collection. The stair down to the collective living spaces plays against the subtle drama of the angled south facade, to draw you to the desert beyond; the double-height living room takes you to the sky and horizon.

Photos: © Bill Timmerman

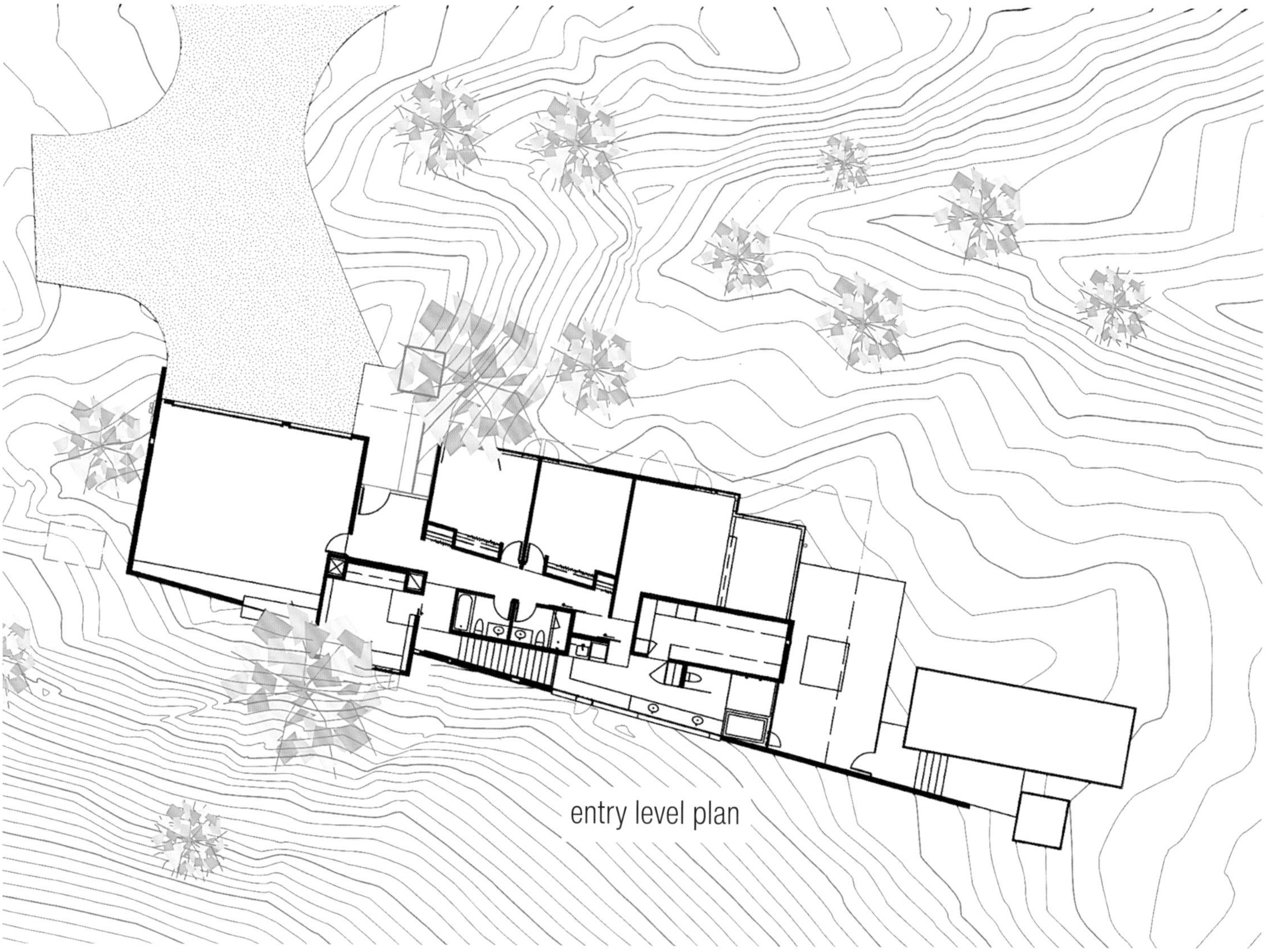

entry level plan

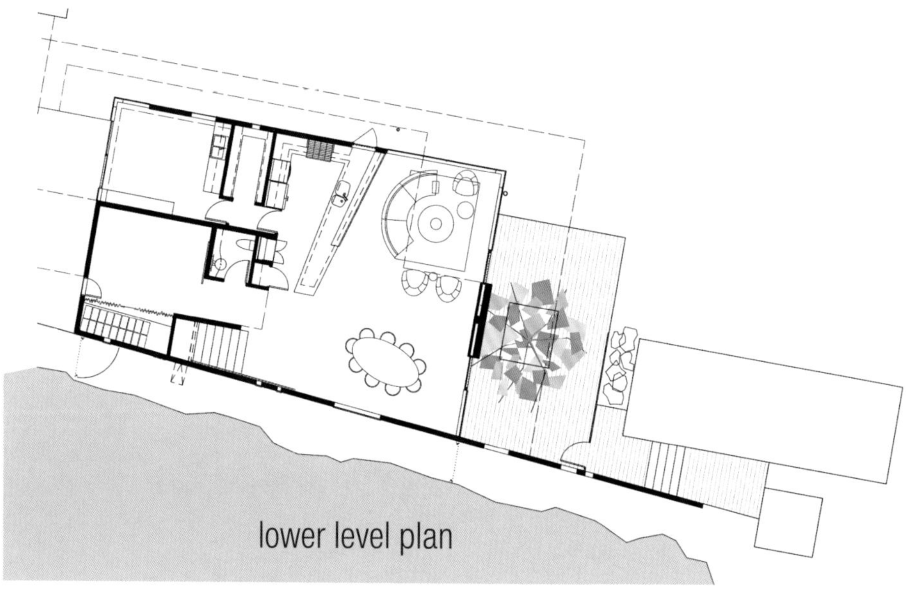

lower level plan

Henkel Headquarters
Scottsdale, Arizona, 2006

Located in a development urban area of Scottsdale, Arizona, the new Henkel Headquarters is an innovative collaborative center, completely integrated into its broader context of the Sonoran Desert. The building is conceived as a crystalline cloud floating over a desert mesa, a graceful presence at the prominent intersection of Scottsdale Road and the 101 Freeway. The four-story structure is comprised of two levels of glass curtain wall, environmentally shaded by a double ceramic frit, above two levels clad in aluminum panels, deeply textured plaster, and native Ash Fork sandstone. From the freeway, its 700-foot south elevation is a 7.5 second experience against the backdrop of the McDowell Mountains. On the north, a casual 7-minute walk moves along its folded facade. As attested to by its LEED certification, Henkel, the original client, took environmental responsibility seriously and believed in its corporate citizenship to provide comfortable and productive working environments. The building makes extensive use of thermal and shading technologies, raised floor systems, and indirect lighting and sensitive use of daylight in office areas.

Photos: © Bill Timmerman

Henkel
Henkel

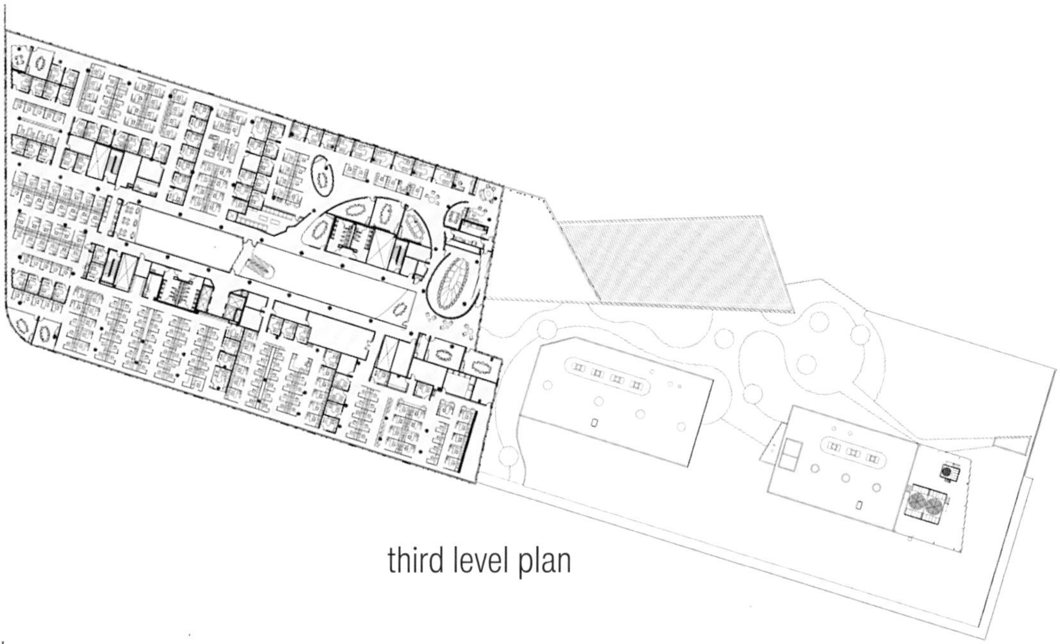

third level plan

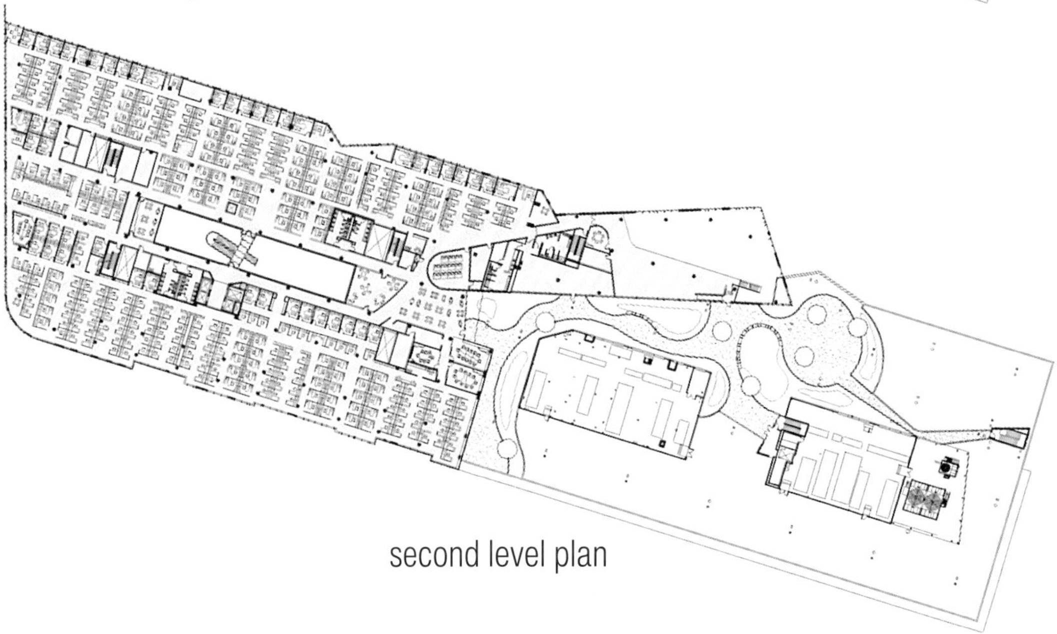

second level plan

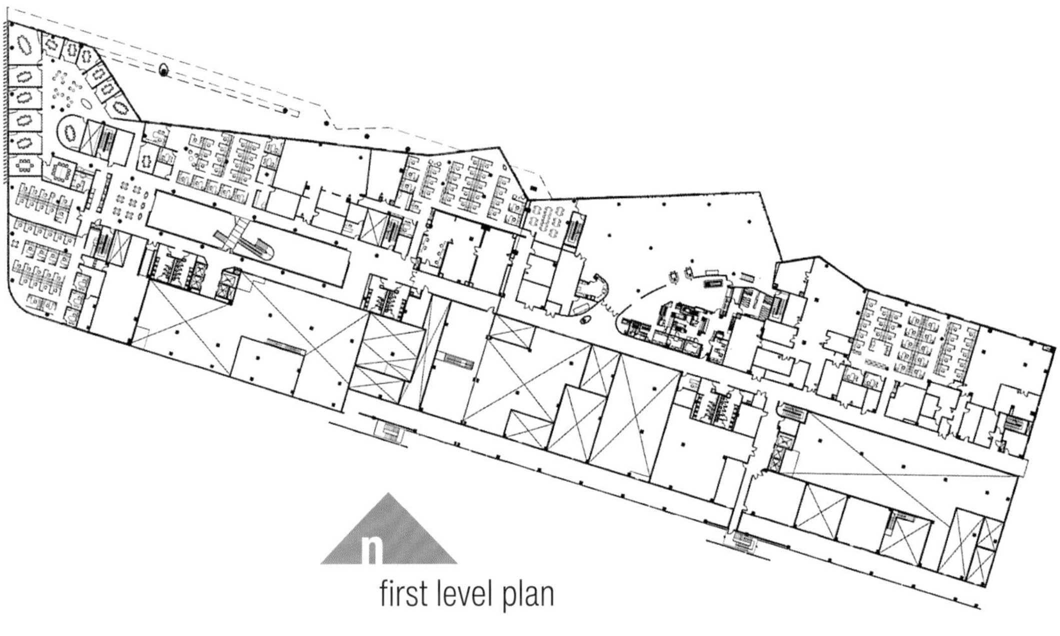

first level plan

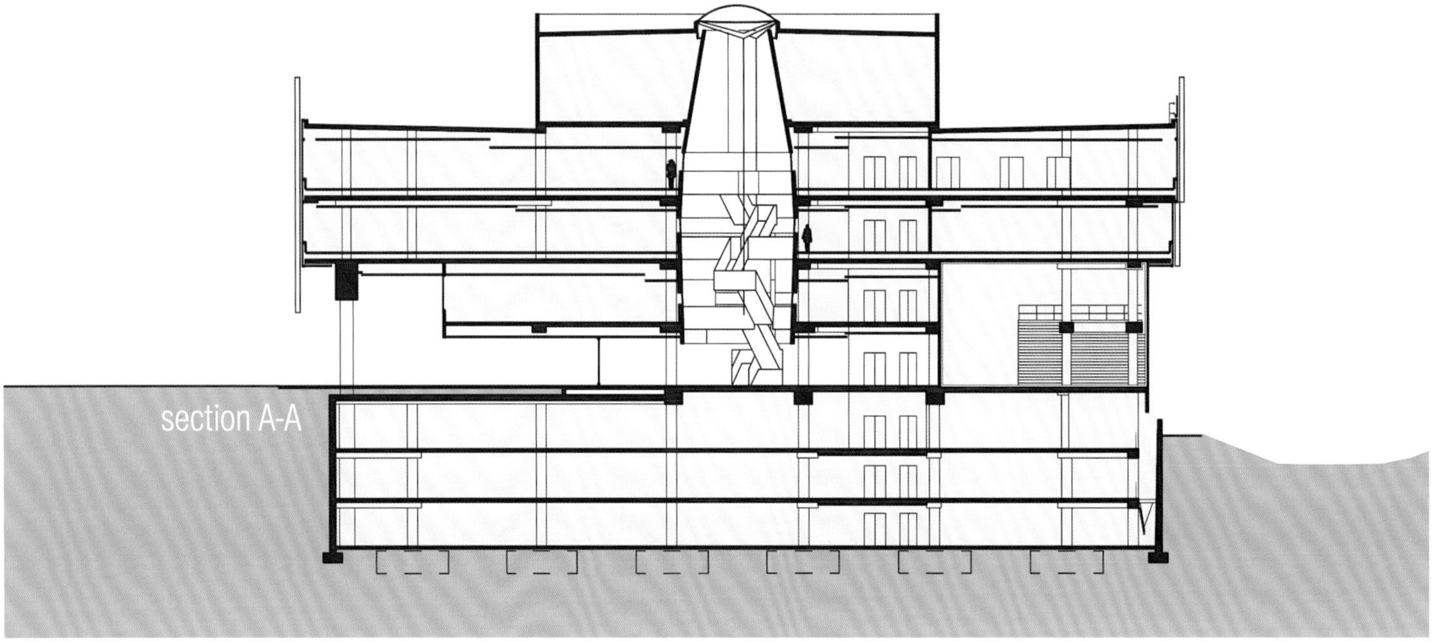
section A-A

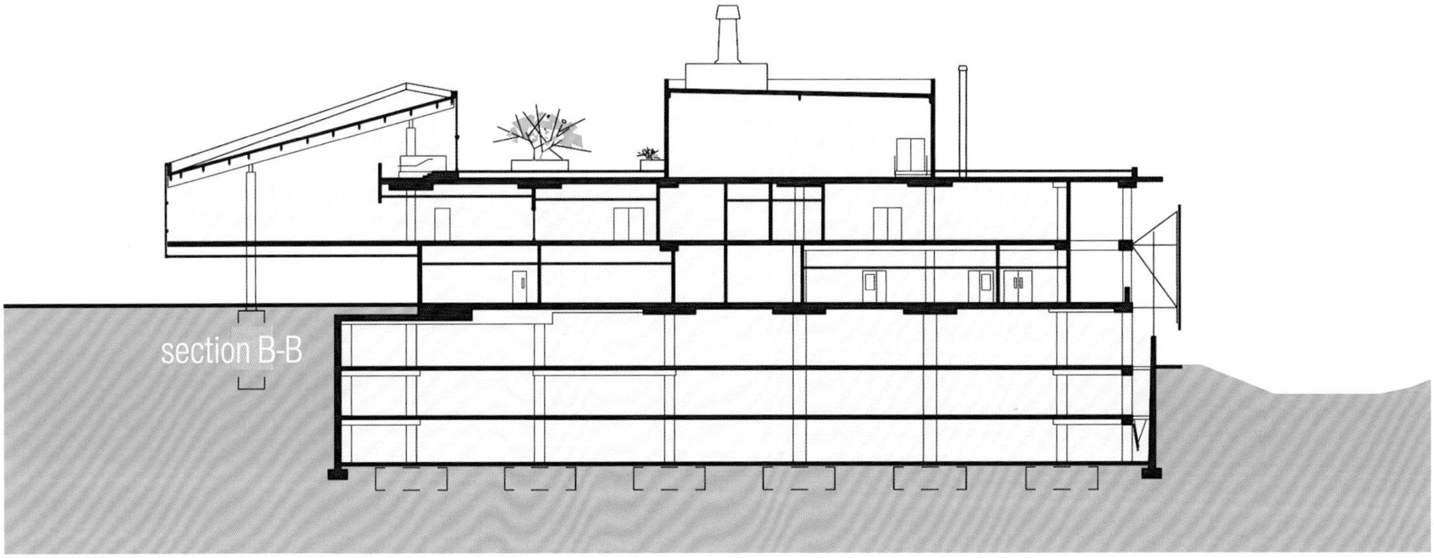
section B-B

Billings Public Library

Billings, Montana, 2010

© Will Bruder

The form and materials of the new Billings Public Library draw from local references, both natural and man-made: the geologic uniqueness of the region's Rimrocks, the "big sky" expansiveness of the horizon and clarity of light, the beautifully austere first settlers' homes and ranch buildings, the modest and simple elegance of Montana pole barns, the statuesque grain elevators, and the long and low storage sheds lining the region's railroads. Fully engaged with the urban context of downtown Billings, the library resonates with the original and beautiful early twentieth-century civic and commercial architecture that lines Montana and Broadway Avenues.

Billings Public Library makes an appropriately grand civic gesture as it rises from a foundation of indigenous Rimrock golden-gray sandstone, capped with a well-proportioned and finely crafted assemblage of zinc-clad wall panels, environmentally responsive glazing systems, and shimmering perforated stainless-steel shading panels that are calibrated to maximize views and optimize light.

Day or night, the subtle transparency and glow of the grand reading room casts the library as a warm and inviting pavilion of public purpose, anchoring the northern edge of downtown Billings.

Achieving a LEED Platinum Certificate in 2015, the library stands out as a standard of affordable sustainability for the community and the region.

Photos: © Bill Timmerman, unless noted

N BROADWAY
BILLINGS PUBLIC LIBRARY
ONLY

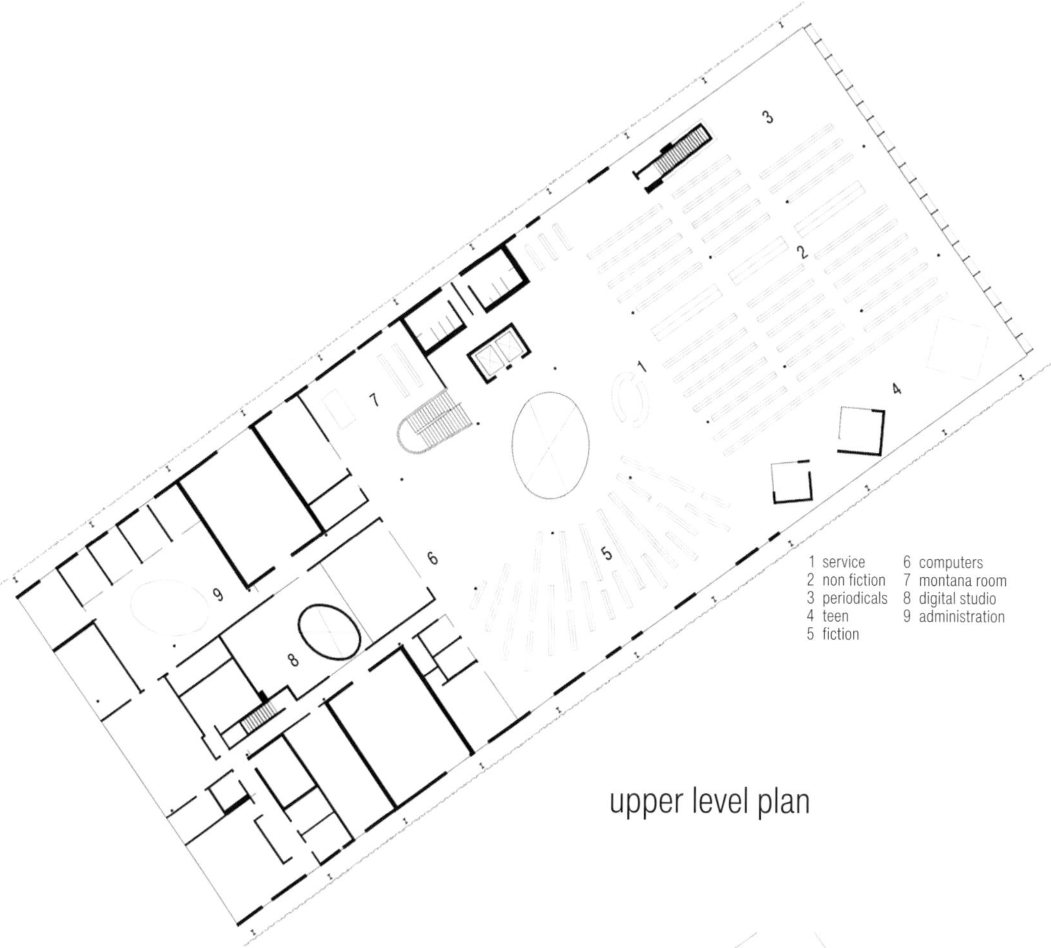

upper level plan

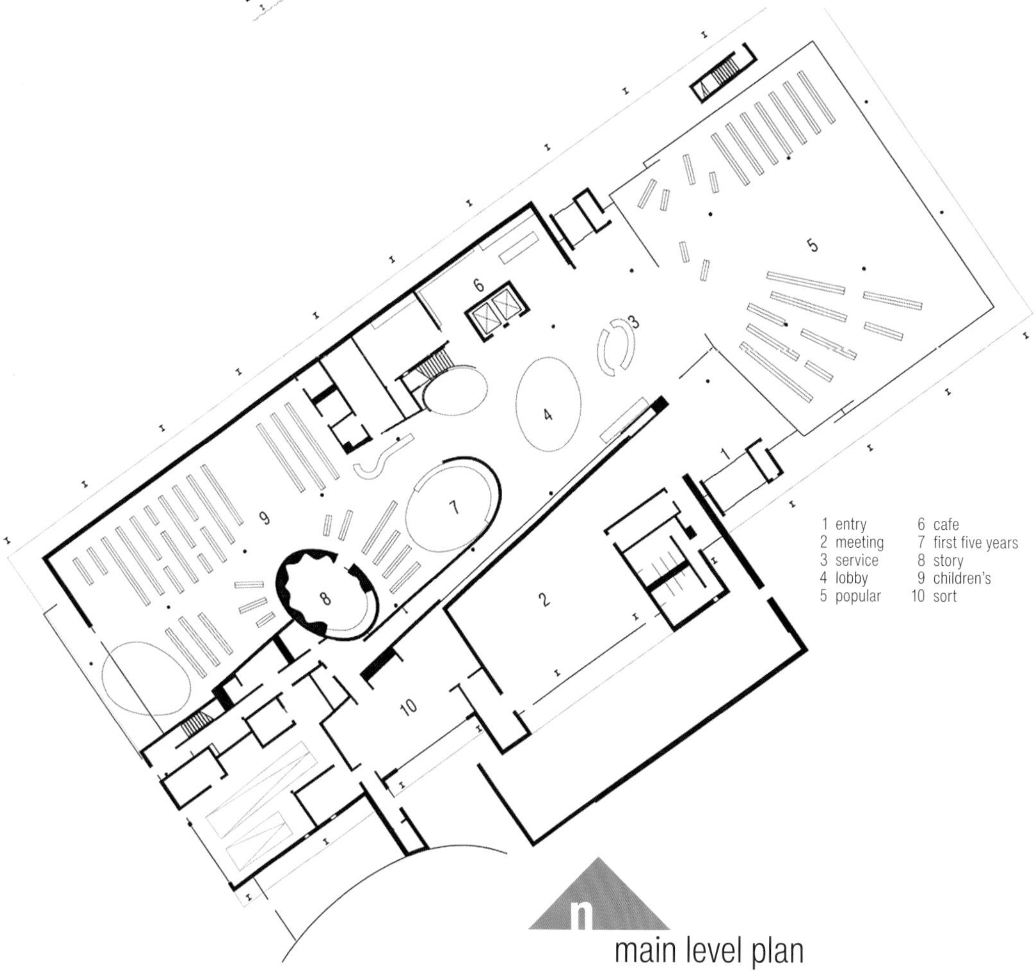

main level plan

BILLINGS PUBLIC LIBRARY

BILLINGS PUBLIC LIBRARY

Reading is a basic tool in the living of a good life.
A poet is, before anything else, a person who is passionately in love with language. W. H. Auden

FICTION
TEENS

EENS

Blackbird House

Aspen, Colorado, 2012

This urban mountain retreat is located on a small cul-de-sac lot, three blocks from the main ski lift in downtown Aspen. The site offers spectacular 360-degree views. In a neighborhood of modest mid-century-modern houses and apartments, the architecture's floor plan and section are a creative response to the town's urban form-based zoning codes. While generous, the project respects a building scale complementary to the community's historic fabric of wood-sided one bedroom miner's cabins and delicately detailed nineteenth century Victorian homes.

The relatively modest cul-de-sac-facing entry is richly detailed with vertical charred (Shou-Sugi-Ban) cypress boards and custom-formed standing-seam Anthra-Zinc metal cladding. Generous window apertures are placed to capture the surrounding views, while the architecture visually recedes into the shadows of the aspen and conifer trees that surround it.

Interior finishes include polished reflective white diamond-troweled plaster walls and ceilings, doors and cabinets of white rift-sawn oak, floors of engineered walnut, large-format porcelain tile or carpet, and fireplaces and bathing chambers clad in thin stone. The architecture is designed to be a rustically refined backdrop for a sophisticated, indoor/outdoor contemporary lifestyle, where all of one's senses are engaged and enhanced throughout the seasons of Aspen.

Photos: © Bill Timmerman

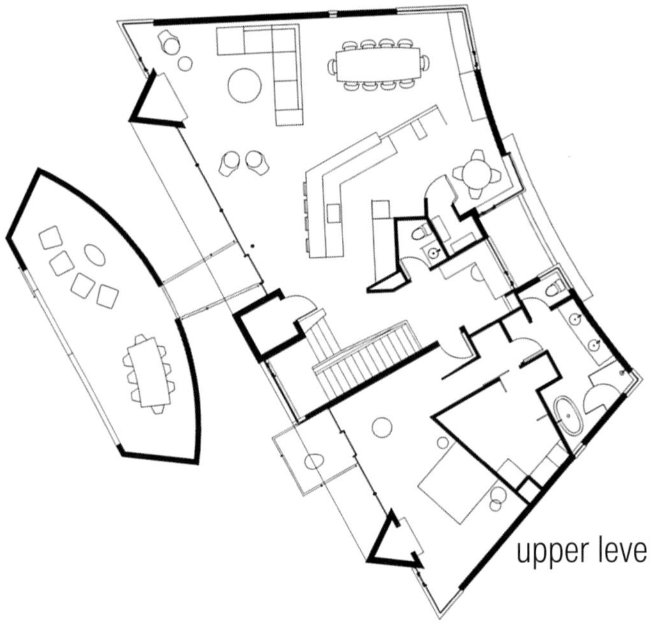

upper level plan

main level plan

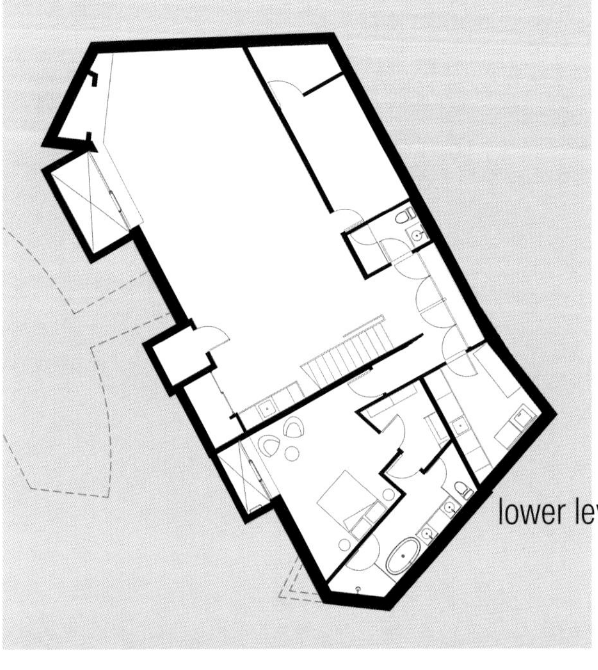

lower level plan

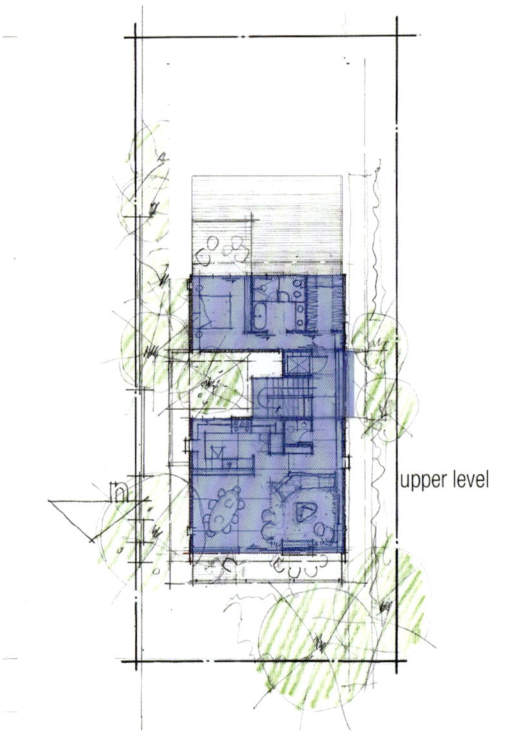

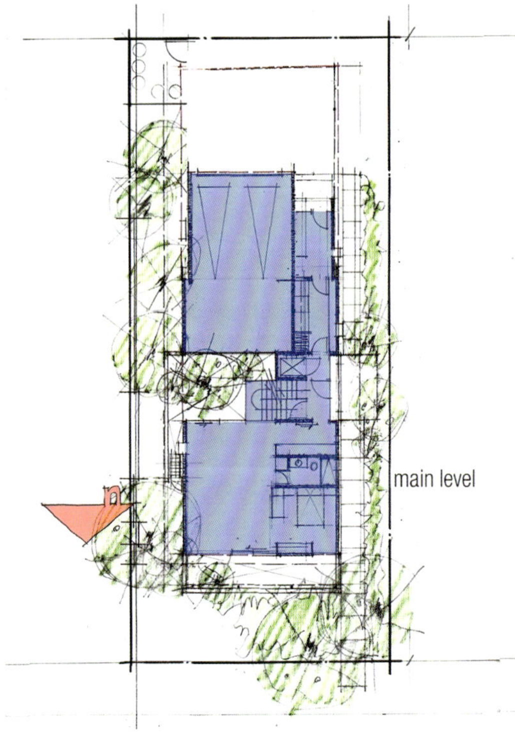

Riddell Residence/Urban

Jackson, Wyoming, 2013

Riddell Urban is a compact two-story residence located on a modest urban lot two blocks from the town square—replete with antler archways—of Jackson, Wyoming. Set on the south side of this urban street, the entry is off a narrow side yard, facing west at the center of the plan. A two-car garage is accessed via an alley to the south. Exterior walls are primarily clad in blackened/burnt 1 ◊ 4 resawn vertical T & G cedar boards (using a Japanese finishing technique), unpainted cement board, or vertical corrugated gray Anthra-Zinc metal cladding. All surfaces reflect the refined scale of the architecture.

Interior finishes include exposed concrete floors, smooth finish drywall, and walnut veneered and dry lacquered cabinetwork with non-directional finished stainless-steel counters. A polished edge on these counters captures available light.

The first-level entry offers a shared den, library, and small studio suite, as well as a fenced terrace looking north to the street.

Photos: © Edward Riddell

J.K. ROWLING
LAST BUS
WISDOM
IVAN
DOIG

Eldorado on 1st

Scottsdale, Arizona, 2013

With its folded skins of bonderized metal and ephemeral railings of perforated pewter-gray steel, Eldorado on 1st is envisaged to be as elusive as the shimmering desert mirage. Further, its randomly offset stack bond masonry creates an architecture of ever-changing, complex shadows, recalling the classic modernism of the Arizona Biltmore Hotel, the post-Taliesin West desert designs of Frank Lloyd Wright, and the much-celebrated modern design ideals at the core of Scottsdale's defining mid-century period of growth.

The four-story concrete, masonry, steel, and glass structure contains seven townhouse-style dwelling units, fronted at street level by commercial office spaces. All principal living areas within are complemented with adjacent outdoor living spaces, culminating in discrete rooftop terraces enhanced with outdoor kitchens, fire features, and native plantings. The cores of the dwellings are imbued with daylight through the delicately detailed stair towers and focused light wells of frosted glass that at night transform adjacent spaces with their glowing lantern-like appearance.

The play of light continues with *Four Point Line* by artist Jay Atherton, a polished stainless-steel ribbon set into the concrete sidewalk, which demarcates the public/private threshold and offers visitors and pedestrians a river of reflections as they traverse the site.

Carefully calibrated in its use of proportion and scale, Eldorado on 1st is a finely-grained urban composition that is designed to quietly and distinctively complement the walkable pedestrian environment of downtown Scottsdale.

Photos: © Bill Timmerman

EXIT

1005

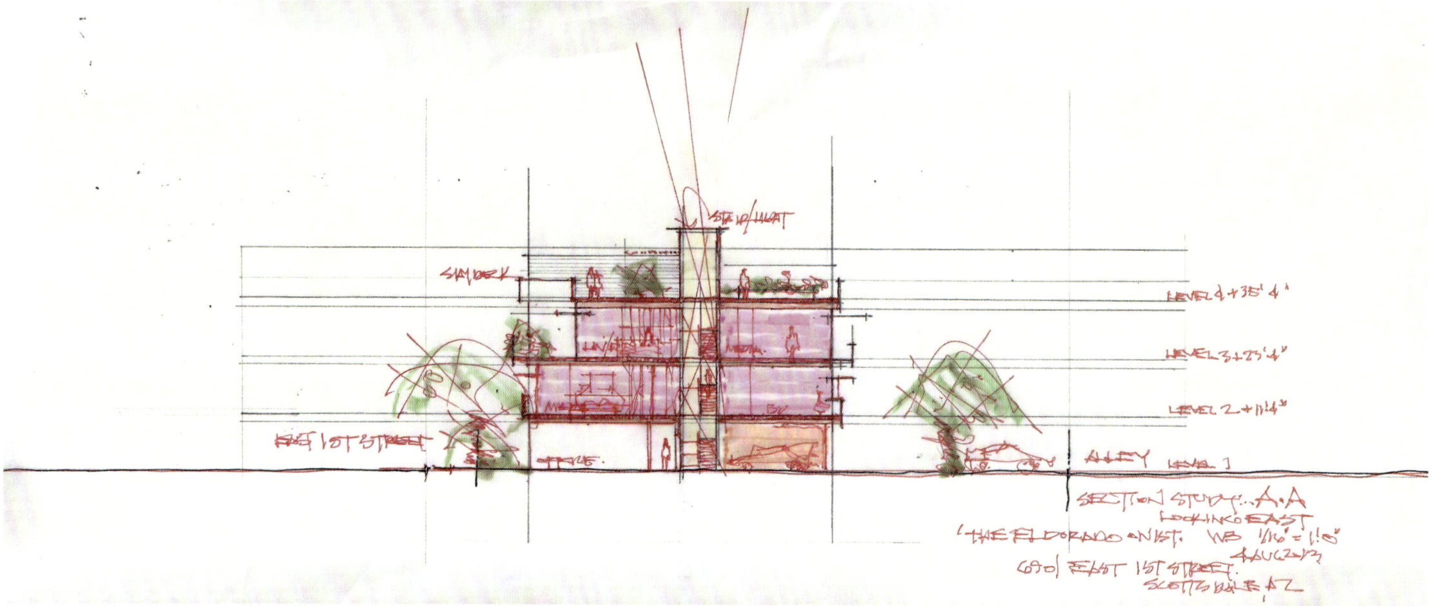

EAST 1ST STREET
LEVEL 4 +35'4"
LEVEL 3 +23'4"
LEVEL 2 +11'4"
ALLEY
LEVEL 1
SECTION STUDY... A·A
LOOKING EAST
'THE ELDORADO ON 1ST.' WB 1/16" = 1'0"
6901 EAST 1ST STREET.
SCOTTSDALE AZ

PALMtower

Phoenix, Arizona, 2024

Rising from the northwest corner of East Van Buren and North 5th Street, the twenty-one residential levels of PALMtower appear to float above the seven-level podium embraced by majestic palm trees and desert landscaping. Wrapped in translucent metallic scrim and ribbons of glass, the podium welcomes residents into an expressive eighteen-foot-tall lobby. The transparent facade of the ground floor promotes dynamic daylit spaces that visually connect the energy of the street and residential amenity spaces to the enclosed gardens beyond. The interior finishes are earnest and tactile and include polished concrete, metals, terracotta, resin, and woods.

The podium is capped by a full amenity floor to include an outdoor pool, spa, and private gardens. The material palette resonates with the ground floor with transparent facades that invite, and allow for tracking the seasonal path of the sun from first light to sunset and dusk.

Residential apartments with varied living configurations and balcony arrangements hover above the podium, each with a uniquely expansive skyline view. PALMtower—as it catches light, sculpts shadow and refracts color—presides as a distinctive sculptural gesture marking the heart of the reemerging downtown on the Phoenix skyline.

Photos: © Bill Timmerman

Van Buren
Arizona Center
Children's Museum

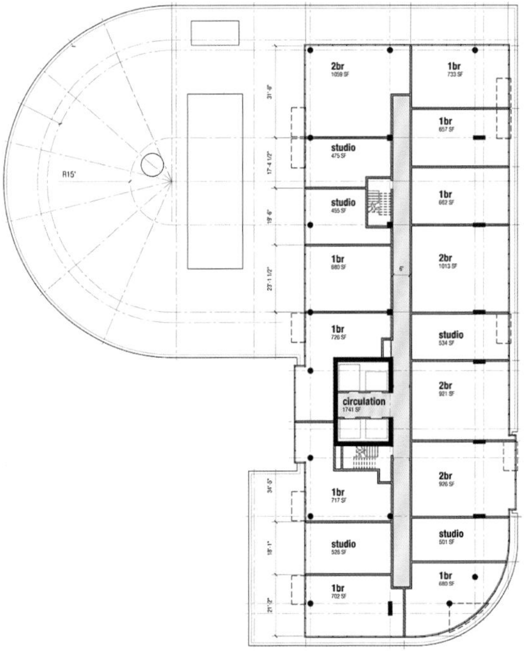

typical floor plan 8-28

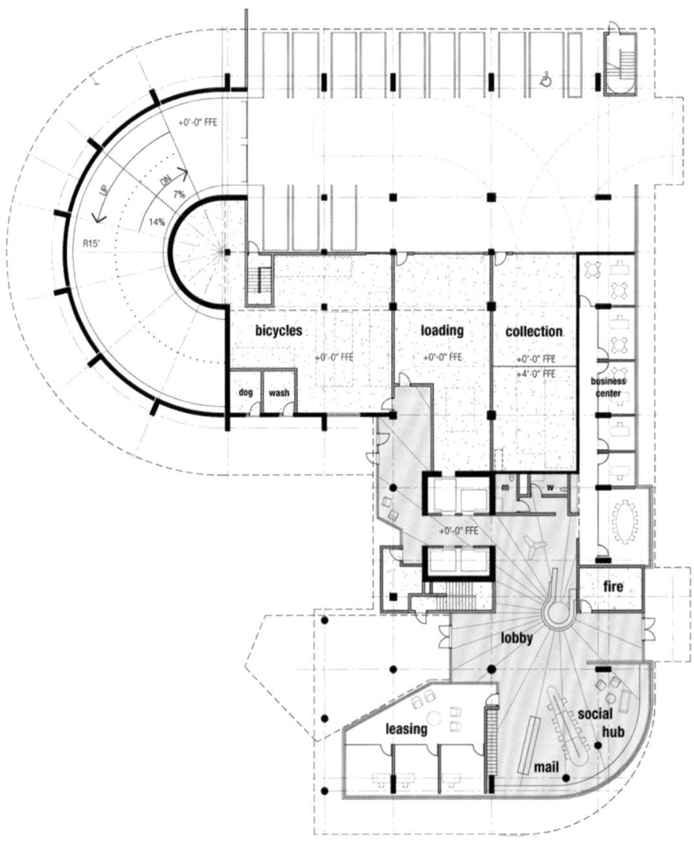

main level plan

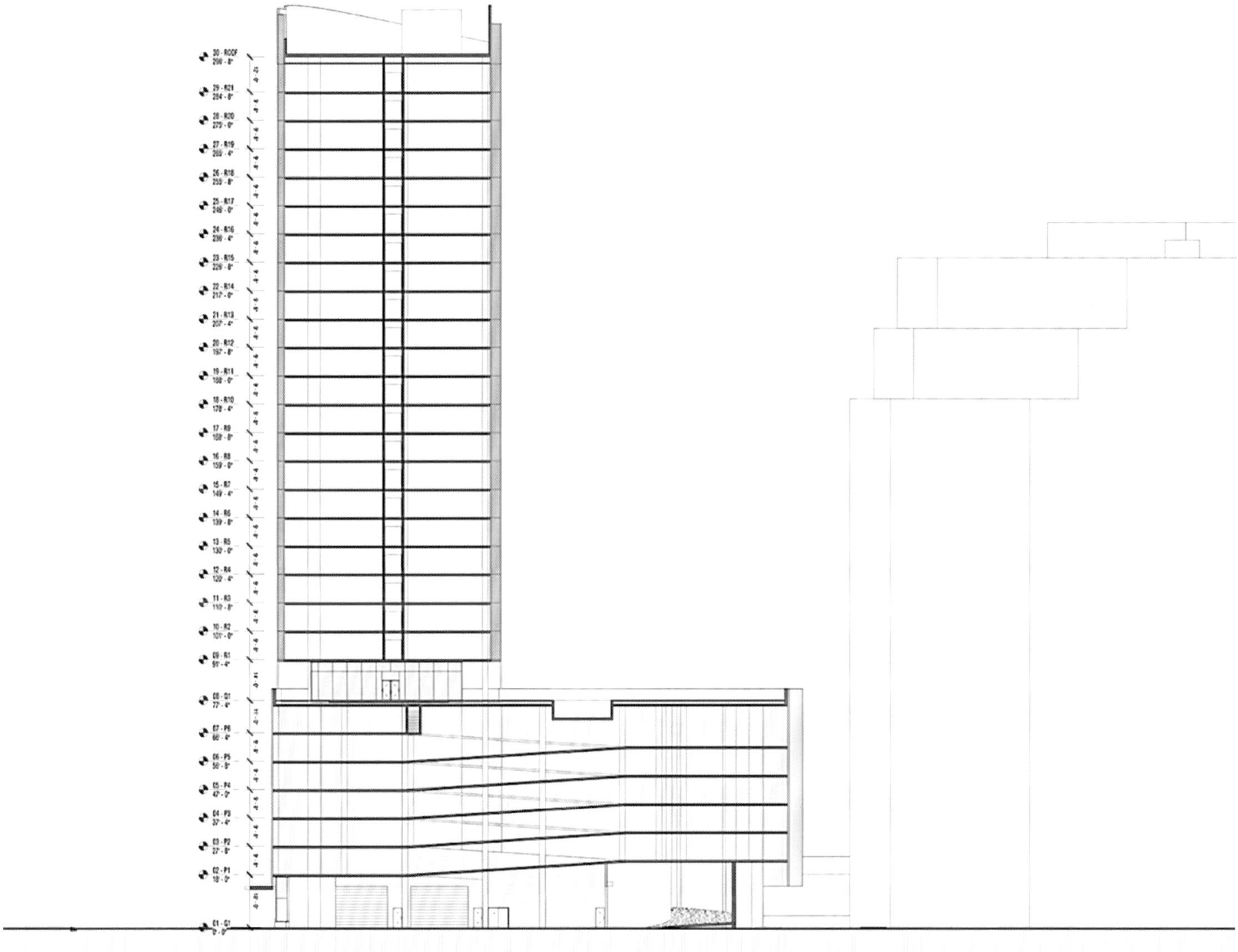

section A-A

MATRIX

Architectural design excellence...

When we experience architectural design excellence all our senses are alerted and nourished.

Our curiosity is piqued, our time and place is reflected and respected in unexpected ways.

Our minds are opened to new ideas, our confidence in the possibility of the human endeavor renewed.

We feel comfortable yet challenged, understood yet urged to stretch.

We want to be in such places alone and together with others.

We want to be in such places at all times of day and night and through all seasons.

We want time in such places to learn their secrets and confirm the validity of our initial awe.

We want such places to serve as markers of our best efforts.

We want such places to exist beyond our lifetime.

AIA National Design Excellence Committee–2011

appendix

Selected Project List

Italic for unbuilt project.

1971 - 1974 William P. Bruder Environmental Design

1971 Facings of America Showroom, Phoenix, Arizona
Van Gilse Remodel/Addition, Phoenix, Arizona

1972 Caldwell Patio, Phoenix, Arizona
Croom Entry Remodel, Phoenix, Arizona
Galloway Patios, Glendale, Arizona
Neely Showroom Remodel, Phoenix, Arizona
Paul Schweikher/Architect ASU Exhibit, Tempe, Arizona

1973 Galloway Cabin, Pinewood, Arizona
Loper Residence, Chandler, Arizona
Matthews Residence Addition, Tempe, Arizona
Rotharmel Patio, Glendale, Arizona

1974 - 1999 William P. Bruder Architect Ltd.

1974 Irwin Remodel and Patio, Phoenix, Arizona
JI Bammerlin Credit Union, Phoenix, Arizona
Spotnitz Residence, Paradise Valley, Arizona
U-Cart Concrete Facility I, Phoenix, Arizona

1975 Fig Tree Patio, Phoenix, Arizona
Will Bruder Studio/Residence, New River, Arizona
Karber A/C Offices, Phoenix, Arizona
King Residence Remodel, Phoenix, Arizona
Lawson Patios, Phoenix, Arizona
Rotharmel Studio Retreat, Glendale, Arizona

1976 Caslake Remodel, Phoenix, Arizona
Kovach Solar Residence, Spring Valley, Arizona
Lawson Residence Remodel, Phoenix, Arizona
Topliff Patio, Phoenix, Arizona

1977 Clark Residence Remodel, Phoenix, Arizona
Karber Residence, Phoenix, Arizona
Peters Residence, Tempe, Arizona
Platt Residence, Phoenix, Arizona
Ross Residence, Cave Creek, Arizona

1978 Bates Residence, Phoenix, Arizona
Deberdt Residence, Monterey, California
Lomas Housing Compound, Phoenix, Arizona
Matthews Residence, Phoenix, Arizona
Russell Remodel and Patios, Phoenix, Arizona
Streech Residence Remodel, Tempe, Arizona
Wooton Residence, Tacna, Arizona
Maude's An Eating Establishment, Prescott, Arizona

1979 Mesquite Branch Library, Phoenix, Arizona
Will Bruder Studio Expansion, New River, Arizona
Streech Office Remodel, Phoenix, Arizona
Johnston Residence, Phoenix, Arizona
1980 *Dewayne Matthews Residence, Santa Fe, New Mexico*
Lawson Guest House/Cabana/Pool, Phoenix, Arizona
Phetteplace Residence, Prescott, Arizona
Smith Residence, Phoenix, Arizona
Johnson Residence, Black Canyon City, Arizona
1981 Koppes Residence Addition, Phoenix, Arizona
Lamoure Residence, New River, Arizona
Loba Lodge Cabin, Yavapai County, Arizona
Nelson Residence, Prescott, Arizona
North Scottsdale Methodist Church, Scottsdale, Arizona
Phoenix Day School for the Deaf Gym/Auditorium, Phoenix, Arizona
Rosenbaum Residence, Cave Creek, Arizona
1982 Karber A/C Offices Remodel/Addition, Phoenix, Arizona
Streech Electric Expansion/Pilcher Building, Phoenix, Arizona
1983 *Arndt Residence, Paulden, Arizona*
Bruder Exhibit/Tempe Art Museum, Tempe, Arizona
Farnham Residence Remodel, Phoenix, Arizona
Heede Residence, Scottsdale, Arizona
Pulis Residence, Scottsdale, Arizona
Redman Residence, Tempe, Arizona
1984 Auto Shack I Prototype, Glendale, Arizona
Ferris/Lacey Residence, Phoenix, Arizona
Glenn Residence, Phoenix, Arizona
Mirage Fashion Salon Remodel, Scottsdale, Arizona
Rotharmel Residence, Monterey, California
Saguaro Branch Library Remodel, Phoenix, Arizona
1985 *Arizona Heritage Center Competition, Tempe, Arizona*
Collier Residence, Phoenix, Arizona
Graham Foundation Exhibit, Chicago, Illinois
North Arizona University Honors College, Flagstaff, Arizona
Toone Spec/La Casa Victoria Nueva Residence, Mesa, Arizona
Weiss Residence, Paradise Valley, Arizona
1986 Cholla Branch Library, Phoenix, Arizona
Cosaboom/Fitzsimons Residence, Scottsdale, Arizona
CRB Mechanical Insulation, Phoenix, Arizona
Eichorn Residence, Big Sur, California

Farman Residence Addition, Paradise Valley, Arizona
Nykamp Remodel, Paradise Valley, Arizona
Verde Valley School Plan, Sedona, Arizona
1987 Silverman Remodel, Phoenix, Arizona
Weiss Guys Car Wash, Glendale, Arizona
Nellis Cox Residence, Cave Creek, Arizona
1988 Deer Valley Petroglyph Preserve, Glendale, Arizona
Karber/Interstate Mechanical Expansion/IMCOR, Phoenix, Arizona
Karaszewski Residence, Zion Park, Utah
Lawson Residence Remodel, Phoenix, Arizona
Lighting Dynamics Studio, Phoenix, Arizona
Murray Residence, New River, Arizona
1989 Phoenix Central Library, Phoenix, Arizona
bruderDWLarchitects
Pfeiffer Residence, Glenwood Springs, Colorado
Smith Residence, Tucson, Arizona
Theuer Residence, Ahwatukee, Arizona
Zeitlen Residence, Phoenix, Arizona
1990 Hill Sheppard Residence, Phoenix, Arizona
Nunn Entry Remodel, Phoenix, Arizona
1991 Bruder Workshop/Studio Remodel, New River, Arizona
Equiaid Headquarters, Phoenix, Arizona
1992 Teton County Public Library, Jackson, Wyoming
Temple Kol Ami, Scottsdale, Arizona
Arizona Public Service Showcase Home Competition, Phoenix, Arizona
Bass Residence, Tucson, Arizona
Farnham Residence Remodel, Phoenix, Arizona
Rosensteel Residence Remodel, Phoenix, Arizona
Schweikher Residence Remodel, Phoenix, Arizona
1993 *Habitat for Humanities Housing, Phoenix, Arizona*
Horne Residence, Sea Arc, Prides Crossing, Massachusetts
Riddell Advertising, Jackson, Wyoming
Ruff Residence Remodel, Scottsdale, Arizona
1994 Byrne Residence, Scottsdale, Arizona
Townsend Residence, Paradise Valley, Arizona
1995 Mad River Rafting, Jackson, Wyoming
San Diego Public Library Competition, San Diego, California
Black Canyon Restaurant, New York, New York
Burian Residence, New River, Arizona

1996 Costello Residence, Mesa, Arizona
Dumoulin/Emanuel Addition, Anchorage, Alaska
Scottsdale Museum of Contemporary Art (SMoCA), Scottsdale, Arizona
1997 *Linde Residence/Museum, Paradise Valley, Arizona*
Salt Lake City Library Feasibility Study, Salt Lake City, Utah
1998 Heller Residence, Ridgway, Colorado
ASU Mediated Classroom Building, Tempe, Arizona
Salt Lake City Library Competition, Salt Lake City, Utah
SMoCA Bruder Exhibit, Scottsdale, Arizona
1999 Kursh Piccioni Residence, Sky Arc, Marin County, California
Nevada Museum of Art (NMA), Reno, Nevada
Riddell Residence/Rural, Wilson, Wyoming
New School for the Arts, Tempe, Arizona

2000 - 2006 Will Bruder Architects Ltd

2000 James Turrell "Knight Rising" Skyspace/SMoCA, Scottsdale, Arizona
Urban Design Guidelines for RTA/Light Rail, Phoenix/Tempe/Mesa, Arizona
2001 111 W Monroe Elevator Lobby East Facade, Phoenix, Arizona
Las Cruces Courthouse GSA Competition, Las Cruces, New Mexico
Madison Central Library Expansion Competition, Madison, Wisconsin
in collaboration with HGA Architects
2002 Pond House, Cave Creek, Arizona
The Vale, Tempe, Arizona
Loloma 5, Scottsdale, Arizona
Minneapolis Central Library Competition, Minneapolis, Minnesota
in collaboration with HGA Architects
2003 *Colorado Springs K-12 School Competition, Colorado Springs, Colorado*
Feigin Residence, Reno, Nevada
Hercules Public Library, Hercules, California
Pool Residence, Reno, Nevada
2004 Agave Branch Library, Phoenix, Arizona
TAXI, Denver, *Colorado*
in collaboration with David Baker + Partners & Harry Teague Architects
2005 *W Hotel, Phoenix, Arizona*
American Craft Museum Competition, New York, New York
ASU Arts and Business Gateway, Tempe, Arizona
ASU Downtown Master Plan, Phoenix, Arizona
Biblioteca de México Competition, Mexico City, Mexico
Jarson Residence, Paradise Valley, Arizona
Mezzo, Phoenix, Arizona
211 Tower Proposal, Phoenix, Arizona

2006 - 2012 Will Bruder + Partners Ltd.

2006 Will Bruder + Partners Ltd. Urban Studio, Phoenix, Arizona
Henkel Headquarters, Scottsdale, Arizona
Tatweer Iconic Towers Design, Saudi Arabia

2007 *Bail Casey Residence Remodel, Paradise Valley, Arizona*
The Roark Multi-Family Housing, Phoenix, Arizona

2008 Bridget Hall-Gilbert Chandler Community College, Mesa, Arizona
CBD101 Mixed-Use Master Plan, Glendale, Arizona
Mohave County Public Library, Bullhead City, Arizona

2009 Built-Unbuilt ASU Bruder Exhibit, Tempe, Arizona

2010 Billings Public Library, Billings, Montana
in collaboration with O2 Architects
Arizona State Capitol Centennial 2012 Plan + 2020 Vision, Phoenix, Arizona
in collaboration with AIA/ASU/ASLA

2011 James Turrell "Air Apparent" Sky Space, ASU, Tempe, Arizona
Kimball Art Center Competition, Park City, Utah

2012 - present Will Bruder Architects LLC

2012 Blackbird House, Aspen, Colorado
Ingo's Tasty Food, Phoenix, Arizona
Moran Loft Remodel, Phoenix, Arizona

2013 Eldorado on 1st, Scottsdale, Arizona
Greiner Residence, Sky Walk, Prides Crossing, Massachusetts
Riddell Residence/Urban, Jackson, Wyoming
Phoenix Center for the Arts (PCA) North Performance Space, Phoenix, Arizona

2014 R&D Residence Remodel, Tempe, Arizona
Shipping Containers 7 Housing, Phoenix, Arizona

2015 *Bryan Park 3, Reno, Nevada*
Hu Residence, Trampoline House, Paradise Valley, Arizona
Horizon on Central Mixed-Use Tower, Phoenix, Arizona
Kinetik I.T. Inc. Remodel, Phoenix, Arizona
2016 Atkins Residence, Palms Tree House, Phoenix, Arizona
Dow Residence, Compass House, Yarnell, Arizona

2020 Paul Schweikher Architect Monograph Draft
in collaboration with Richard Emanuel

2024 PALMtower, Phoenix, Arizona
in collaboration with Lamar Johnson Collaborative

2025 Nevada Museum of Art Expansion, Reno, Nevada
in collaboration with Lamar Johnson Collaborative

Selected Books

Reimagine the Library of the Future, Steffen Lehmann, ORO Editions 2022
Wunderkammer, Tod Williams and Billie Tsien, Yale University Press 2013
Architecture Now Houses, Philip Jodidio, Taschen—June 2009
Modern Architecture A-Z, Peter Gossel Ed., Taschen—2007
PHX: Phoenix 21st Century City, by Edward Booth-Clibborn, Booth-Clibborn Editions—2006
New Museums: Contemporary Museum Architecture around the World, by Raul A. Barreneche, Phaidon—2011
Modern House 3, by Raul A. Barreneche, Phaidon Press—2005
Modern American Houses: Fifty Years of Design in Architectural Record, by Clifford A. Pearson, Abrams—2005
Jewish Identity in Contemporary Architecture, by Angeli Sachs Ed. and Edward van Voolen Ed., Prestel—2004
American Synagogues, by Samuel Gruber et al., Rizzoli—2003
Ten: A Decade of Design, by Chrysler Design Awards—2002
Modern House 2, The Byrne Residence, the Editors of Phaidon Press, Phaidon Press—2000
Designing the New Museum, by James Grayson Trulove, Rockport Publishers—2000
Building a New Millennium, by Philip Jodidio, Taschen—1999
Phoenix Central Library, by Oscar Riera Ojeda Ed. and Nader Tehrani, Single Building Series, Rockport Publishers—1999
Library Builders, by Michael Brawne, Academy Editions—1997
The Architecture of Museums, by Hearst Books International, Arco Publishing—1997
Contemporary American Architects: Volume II, by Philip Jodidio, Taschen—1996
"Cowboy Front for Culture," C3, Publisher Jaehong Lee, July 2010
"A Dialogue with Editor-Will Bruder" & "Jarson Residence" GA Houses 116, Editor Yoshio Futagawa, May 2010
"Will Bruder: Feigin Residence & Pool Residence," GA Houses 102, Editor Yoshio Futagawa, November 2007
"William Bruder: Sky Arc Residence," GA Houses 87, Editor Yoshio Futagawa, April 2005
"Hill Sheppard Residence," интерьер дайджест (Interior Digest), Андрей Чирков (Andrey Chirkov), April 2004
"William Bruder: Nevada Museum of Art," GA Document 75, Editor Yoshio Futagawa, October 2003
"William P. Bruder: Horne/Thompson Residence," GA Houses Special 02; Masterpieces 1971-2000, Editor Yoshio Futagawa, November 2001

"William P. Bruder: Temple Kol Ami," Lotus International 105, Editor Pierluigi Nicolin, 2000
"William P. Bruder: Thompson Residence," GA Houses 65, Editor Yoshio Futagawa, Nov. 2000
"William P. Bruder," Korean Architects 155, by Korean Architects Publishing July 1997. (Parts 1, 2, 3, 4)
"bruderDWLarchitects: Phoenix Central Library," GA Document 46, Editor Yoshio Futagawa, February 1996
"Phoenix Central Library," The Arup Journal, Editor David J. Brown, April 1996
"Monumenten in de uitdijende stad: de architectuur van William Bruder," Aaron Betsky, Archis, July 1996
"William P. Bruder: Horne Residence and Byrne Residence," GA Houses 45; Project 1995, Editor Yoshio Futagawa, March 1995
"Architetture organiche di William Bruder in Arizona," L'Architettura, by Marisa Cerruti, April 1986
"A Special Feature: Friends of Kebyar," A+U: Architecture and Urbanism, by David de Long, March 1985

National Publications

"Residential: Blackbird House," Architect Magazine, by David Hill, August 2015
"Light Defines the Journey of Our Lives," Daylight & Architecture, by Velux Group, Spring 2011
"Public Space," Contract, by Jennifer Thiele Busch, January/February 2010
"Cowboy Modernism," Architectural Record, by Clifford A. Pearson, March 2010
"Henkel Headquarters," Architect Magazine, by Mimi Zeiger, December 2009
"Will Bruder: Artist as Architect," Contract, by Kelly Bauer, July 2008
"Will Bruder," Constructs, by Amy Lelyveld, Spring 2006
"Loloma 5," Architectural Record, by Clifford A. Pearson, July 2005
"Being Bruder," Architecture, July 2003
"The Arizona School," Architecture, by Lawrence Cheek, May 2002
"From Popcorn to Pop Art," Architecture, by Lawrence Cheek, June 1999
"Glazing Arizona," Architectural Review, by Margaret Seal, June 1999
"Record Houses," Architectural Record, by Sarah Amelar, April 1999

"Iron Will," Architecture, by Raul A. Barreneche, September 1997
"William Bruder en Arizona," l'Architecture d'Aujourd'hui, by William Curtis & David Leclerc, October 1996
"Will Bruder Interview," Crit, by John Czarnecki, Fall 1996
"Scarpa in the South-West," Architectural Review, by Margaret Seal, March 1996
"Will Power," Progressive Architecture, by Abby Bussel, July 1995
"Stealth Inscriptions," Architectural Record, by Aaron Betsky, October 1995
"City Libraries: Desert Illumination," Architecture, Editor Deborah K. Dietsch, October 1995
"Desert Classic: Phoenix Central Library," Metropolis, by Reed Kroloff, December 1994
"Desert Shield," Architectural Record, by Clifford A. Pearson, April 1993
"The Shifting Sands," The Los Angeles Times Magazine, by Aaron Betsky, August 1992
"A Desert Lookout" Progressive Architecture, by Philip Arcidi, November 1990
"Reinterpreting Regionalism: Arizona: Three Architects Who Respect the Desert Terrain and Traditions," Architecture: The AIA Journal, by Allen Freeman, March 1984

Local Publications

"Building a New Bruder," The Arizona Republic, by Richard Nilsen, 17 September 2003
"Arizona's Leading Architect Reconsiders the City," Design & Architecture: Arizona Edition, by Dana Hutt, October 2003
"A Balance of Poetry, Pragmatism," The Arizona Republic, by Richard Nilsen, October 1999
"AIA Arizona Homes of the Year," Phoenix: Home & Garden, by Nora Burba Trulsson, May 1992
"AIA Arizona Homes of the Year," Phoenix: Home & Garden, by Nora Burba Trulsson, May 1988

Selected Design Awards

Twenty-five Year Award, AIA National
Burton Barr Phoenix Central Library; Phoenix, AZ—2021

Library Building Award, AIA/ALA
Billings Public Library; Billings, MT—2016

LEED Certification Platinum

Billings Public Library; Billings, MT—2015

LEED Certification Silver Existing Buildings

Burton Barr Phoenix Central Library; Phoenix, AZ—2010

Honor Award, AIA Arizona
Agave Library; Phoenix, AZ—2010

Honor Award, AIA Arizona/Desert Living House of the Year
Jarson Residence; Paradise Valley, AZ—2010

Gold Trowel Award, AZ Masonry Guild - Excellence in Masonry Architectural Awards
Agave Library; Phoenix, AZ—2009

Honor Award, AIA Western Mountain Region
Agave Library; Phoenix, AZ—2009

Architect of the Year, AIA Arizona
Will Bruder—2008

Honor Award, AIA Arizona
TAXI Mixed-Use; Denver, CO—2008

Honor Award, AIA East Bay
Hercules Public Library; Hercules, CA—2007

Honor Award, AIA Northern Nevada/Reno Magazine
Nevada Museum of Art; Reno, NV—2006

Honor Award, AIA Arizona
Nevada Museum of Art; Reno, NV—2004

Artist of the Year, Arizona Governor's Art Award
Will Bruder—2004

Honor Award, AIA Western Mountain Region
Nevada Museum of Art; Reno, NV—2003

Record Home: Award of Excellence for Design, Architectural Record
Byrne Residence; Carefree, AZ—2000

Award in Architecture, American Academy of Arts and Letters—2000

Chrysler Design Award, Chrysler Corporation—2000

Educator of the Year Award, AIA Arizona
Will Bruder—1996

Dupont Benedictus Award, Professional Awards Program-Commercial Use of Glass
Phoenix Central Library; Phoenix, AZ—1996

Honor Award, AIA Arizona
Phoenix Central Library; Phoenix, AZ—1995

Honor Award, AIA Western Mountain Region
Phoenix Central Library; Phoenix, AZ—1995

Honor Award, AIA Arizona Home of the Year
Hill/Sheppard Residence; Phoenix, AZ—1994

Gold Trowel Award, AZ Masonry Guild - Excellence in Masonry Architectural Awards
Weiss Guys Car Wash; Phoenix, AZ—1993

Record Home: Award of Excellence for Design, Architectural Record
Theuer Residence; Phoenix, AZ—1993

Honor Award, AZ Masonry Guild - Excellence in Masonry Architectural Awards
Murray Residence; New River, AZ—1993

Honor Award, AIA Arizona/Phoenix Home & Garden
Murray Residence; New River, AZ—1991

Honor Award, AIA Arizona/Phoenix Home & Garden
Platt Residence; Phoenix, AZ—1989

Honor Award, Metal Construction Association
CRB Mechanical Executive Offices; Phoenix, AZ—1989

Honor Award, AIA Arizona/Phoenix Home & Garden
Weiss Residence; Paradise Valley, AZ—1989

Honor Award, AIA Arizona/Phoenix Home & Garden
Johnston Residence; Phoenix, AZ—1988

Grand National Award, American Car Wash Association
Weiss Guys Car Wash; Chandler, AZ—1987

First Honor Award, American Plywood Association
Galloway Cabin; Pinewood, AZ—1977

Selected Teaching Positions

University of Southern California, Jon Adams Jerde FAIA Distinguished Visiting Professor—Fall 2012

Illinois Institute of Technology, Morgenstern Distinguished Visiting Chair —Spring 2012

Portland State University, Distinguished Visiting Professor of Urban Architecture—2009-2010

University of Oregon, Pietro Belluschi Chair—2008-2009

University of Toronto, Frank Gehry International Visiting Chair—2006

University of New Mexico, Marjorie Mead Hooker Memorial Visiting Professorship—2004

Yale University, William Henry Bishop Professor—2002+2005

University of Virginia, Thomas Jefferson Visiting Professor—2001

University of Oklahoma, Bruce Alonzo Goff Scholar's Chair—1996

Tulane University, Davis Chair—1996

Massachusetts Institute of Technology, Visiting Professor—1996 Spring

Graduate School of Design, Harvard University, Studio Critic—1996

University of New Mexico, Studio Critic—1996

University of Oregon, Summer Studio Critic—1996

New School of Architecture San Diego, CA, Studio Critic—1996

Otaniemi University, 'Cable Works' Campus, Helsinki, Finland, Visiting Professor—1993

Tempe Art Museum, Architectural Workshop for children—1983

University of Arizona, Visiting Professor—1986-1988

Arizona State University, Visiting Professor and critic—1971